Louise Franc

WINTER

Smith
Street
Books

CONTENTS

INTRODUCTION

There's no better place to seek refuge on a rainy day or a cold, blustery evening than the kitchen. It is the warm heart of the home and no more so than in wintertime, when cooking becomes all about comfort foods – slow-cooked meats, rich soups and stews, hearty roasts and fiery curries. It's the time of year to skip the salads and stir-fries and let the art of winter cooking come into its own.

This book is full of recipes to warm you up when you need it most. It features plenty of slow cooking, which helps to add a great depth of flavour and tenderness to dishes, as well as beautiful roasts and incredible vegetable dishes. You'll also find that many of the recipes in this book are one-pot classics. The beauty of these is once you've started the cooking process, there's not much more you'll need to do – except relax and let time do all the work for you.

Because of the longer cooking times, winter recipes lend themselves particularly well to the tougher, but more tasty, cuts of meat – lamb and pork shoulders, stewing beef and beef cheeks and bone-in chicken pieces – which all tend to be less expensive than regular cuts.

We've also included fish and shellfish dishes. Too often overlooked during the cold months, winter is the ideal time to eat seafood – think hearty whole baked fish, rich fish curries or confit salmon paired with winter citrus (page 71) for something lighter.

And of course, no cold-weather meal is complete without something luscious and sweet to finish on. This book has all the decadent and warming desserts you could possibly crave on a cold winter's night.

NOTES ON THE RECIPES

All the recipes in this book give oven temperatures for fan-forced ovens. If you're using a conventional oven, simply increase the temperature by about 10–20°C/30–50°F.

We have used 20 ml (¾ fl oz) tablespoon measures, which is equivalent to 4 teaspoons.

EQUIPMENT

ROASTING TINS

There is truly very little equipment required for oven roasting. One or two deep roasting tins will do the trick – a large one for cooking a whole bird or large joint of meat with veggies, and a smaller one. A good-quality tin with a heavy base will distribute and hold the heat better, and prevent your dish from burning. Beware of roasting tins with fold-away handles – the handles are tricky to fold out again when they are hot, especially when wearing oven gloves.

Your tin should be a maximum of 8 cm (3¼ inches) deep – deep enough to hold liquid safely, but not so deep that it prevents the air circulating around its contents. It should also be large enough to hold your ingredients in one layer; otherwise your food will steam rather than roast.

If you are particularly concerned about fat, you can put your meat or poultry on a rack in the tin, to hold it up above the drippings. This can be useful if you're roasting pork or duck – fattier meats that produce more juices.

OVENPROOF CASSEROLE DISHES AND FRYING PANS

For dishes that need to be covered, a casserole dish with a tight-fitting lid is perfect. A recipe will often stipulate a 'flameproof casserole dish', or sometimes an 'ovenproof frying pan'. This is because the recipe requires ingredients to be browned on the stovetop first and then transferred to the oven. Your dish needs to be tough enough to withstand direct heat to its base; or your frying pan needs to be free of any plastic elements such as handles that might melt in the oven. If you own neither of these, you can use a frying pan to brown your ingredients on the stovetop, then transfer to your casserole dish and place in the oven. It just means dirtying two pots.

THERMOMETERS

Many cooks use a meat thermometer – you can pick one up from any kitchenware shop or even some supermarkets. If you have any worries about the accuracy of your oven, an instant-read thermometer will let you know how your meat is doing. Poke the thermometer 5 cm (2 inches) into the middle of the roast, being careful not to let it touch the bone.

YOUR OVEN

The majority of modern ovens are fan-forced, and these are the temperatures given in the recipes that follow. If you don't have a fan-forced oven, you will need to set the temperature higher than that given. This is usually around 20°C (30–50°F, depending on the fan-forced temperature).

Every oven is different though and, especially if yours is older, you will need to get used to its particular foibles.

You will notice that many pieces of meat or poultry in this book are cooked at a high temperature for a short amount of time, before the oven temperature is reduced; this is to brown the meat before slowly cooking it through.

EXTRAS

It is handy to keep some unwaxed kitchen string in your drawer for trussing meat or chicken. A pair of sharp kitchen scissors or poultry shears are also useful for jointing birds.

COOKING RED MEAT

CUTS OF MEAT

Traditional roasts use the tender meat cuts, such as tenderloin, fillet or ribs, while the tougher cuts usually need longer, slower cooking, often in liquid, to tenderise them. Both types of dish are included in this book: for example, the mini lamb roasts on page 236, and the slow-cooked beef pot roast, made with chuck or blade, on page 187, or the pork knuckle on page 160. Slow-braising in liquid is a great way to tenderise cheaper cuts of meat, which are often full of flavour.

If your meat has the bone still in (for example, a leg of lamb), it will take longer to cook than a boneless piece. A boneless cut will often be rolled and trussed together with string to hold it together and make it a similar thickness throughout for even cooking.

PREPARING THE MEAT

Take your meat out of the fridge about 30 minutes before roasting, so that it comes to room temperature for even cooking. If browning the meat on the stovetop before placing it in the oven, season the meat after you've seared it, as adding salt before you brown it can draw out too much moisture. You might also be instructed to baste the meat during cooking – this simply means spooning some of the pan juices over the meat to keep it moist.

COOKING TIMES

These are given in each recipe but as a rough guide, below are some cooking times per uncooked weight:

Beef: for rare, 20–25 minutes per 500 g (1 lb 2 oz). For medium, 30 minutes per 500 g (1 lb 2 oz).

Lamb: for rare, 20–25 minutes per 500 g (1 lb 2 oz). For medium, 25–30 minutes per 500 g (1 lb 2 oz).

Pork: 30 minutes per 500 g (1 lb 2 oz).

RESTING

When you take roasted meat out of the oven, it is important to let it rest before you carve. Resting cooked meat for around 15 minutes allows it to reabsorb all its juices. If you carve too quickly, the juices will run out all over your carving board and the meat will be dry and tough. Cover the meat loosely with foil (not tightly, or it will steam and overcook under the foil) and leave in a warm place. If you like, you can use this time to make the gravy. Just like basting, resting the meat is all about keeping it as juicy as possible.

To carve, place a damp cloth under your board to ensure that it doesn't move around. Use a carving fork to hold the rested roast in place, and slice across the grain of the meat at a consistent angle with a very sharp carving knife. Stack the slices of meat on a warmed plate as you carve, so that they retain their juices and don't go cold.

ROASTING VEGETABLES AROUND THE MEAT

Meat will usually take longer to cook than vegetables. So get the meat in first, then prepare the vegetables to go around it. They need to be cut into similar-sized pieces so they cook at the same rate. Always use a large enough roasting tin so that your vegetables are not crammed together, causing them to steam rather than crisp up.

Vegetables that roast well include potatoes (an all-rounder variety, such as desiree or sebago), sweet potato, pumpkin, turnip, parsnip, whole carrots, beetroot and onions. These all need around 1 hour in the oven. Fennel – a large bulb cut into quarters should take 30–45 minutes in the oven.

Cooking a great meal is all about timing. Everything needs to come together at the same time: meat, veggies, gravy and side dishes. When you are working out your vegetable cooking times, don't forget you will rest the meat for 15–20 minutes before serving, and that your vegetables can finish off cooking during this time. So if your roast needs 2 hours in the oven and your potatoes and onions need 1 hour, add them to the roasting tin when the meat has been cooking for 1 hour 20 minutes. Once the meat has been removed from the tin, you can turn up the oven for the last minutes of the cooking time so that the potatoes get a good crisp finish. If you are making gravy, move the vegetables to a new baking tray and pop them back in the oven to crisp up while you use the roasting tin to make the gravy.

MAKING GRAVY

For traditional gravy, spoon off all but 2 tablespoons of the meat juices from the roasting tin. Put the roasting tin on the stovetop over low heat and stir about 1 tablespoon of plain (all-purpose) flour into the pan juices. Stir with a wooden spoon over the heat for a couple of minutes to 'cook' the flour, scraping up all the bits from the bottom of the roasting tin. Then start to stir in stock, water or vegetable cooking water, a cupful at a time, stirring well until the liquid is absorbed and there are no lumps. You will need around four cupfuls of liquid, depending on how thick or thin you like your gravy. Once you have added all the liquid, simmer the gravy, stirring occasionally, for 8–10 minutes until reduced and thickened.

COOKING POULTRY

GOLDEN RULES FOR POULTRY

Raw or undercooked poultry can be a potential cause of food poisoning if it is treated carelessly. If you are using frozen chicken, always thaw it thoroughly in the fridge, rather than leaving it out at room temperature. And once it is thawed, use it within 24 hours. When you have prepared raw poultry, always wash the chopping board, knives and other utensils thoroughly in hot soapy water. Don't ever carve the cooked chicken on the unwashed board where you handled it raw.

TRUSSING

If a chicken isn't stuffed then it should be trussed for roasting; otherwise the breast cavity gapes open and hot air can circulate inside, causing the breasts to cook faster than the legs and wings, which can make the breast meat dry out. Trussing simply means tying the legs together with unwaxed kitchen string to keep the cavity closed. Rinse inside the cavity before trussing, and tuck the wing tips under the bird at the same time.

STUFFING

Flavours such lemon, garlic, onion, sage, thyme and other herbs are often used to stuff a bird. A traditional bread stuffing absorbs some of the delicious juices of the meat, while also infusing the bird with the flavourings. If you don't want to serve stuffing with your roast, then simply put your flavourings of choice such as herbs, sliced lemon or onion inside the cavity before trussing.

An alternative to stuffing the bird is to loosen the skin over the breasts by sliding your finger under the skin and running it up and down to detach it from the flesh. Then spread some flavoured butter into the gap between the skin and breasts.

TESTING YOUR BIRD

Overcooking poultry will cause it to dry out, but undercooked poultry can be dangerous. There are many different methods for cooking chicken and turkey – some cooks prefer faster cooking at a higher temperature; others, the opposite – but as a rough guide, a stuffed chicken needs about 30 minutes per 500 g (1 lb 2 oz) in a 180°C (350°F) fan-forced oven. Whatever cooking method you use, to test if your roast bird is ready, insert a skewer into the thickest part of the thigh. When the juices run clear with no sign of pink, it is cooked through. Remove from the oven, cover the bird loosely with foil and leave to rest for around 15 minutes before carving. As with meat, resting the bird lets the juices reabsorb into the meat. Some people leave it to rest upside down so that the juices all run into the breast meat, which can be a little drier.

SOUP

CLASSIC FRENCH ONION SOUP

SERVES 6

2 tablespoons olive oil
50 g (1¾ oz) butter
3 brown onions, thinly sliced
3 red onions, thinly sliced
3 white onions, thinly sliced
½ teaspoon soft brown sugar
250 ml (8½ fl oz/1 cup) dry white wine
1 litre (34 fl oz/4 cups) good-quality
　chicken stock
1 bay leaf
2 tablespoons Cognac, dry vermouth
　or dry sherry
200 g (7 oz/1½ cups) grated gruyère
　or other melting cheese

CROUTONS

sourdough baguette, cut into 12 thick slices
2 tablespoons olive oil

Heat the olive oil and butter in a large heavy-based saucepan over medium heat. Add the onions and stir to coat in the oil and butter mixture. Reduce the heat to low, then cover and cook for 30 minutes, stirring occasionally.

Stir in the sugar and wine. Cover and cook for a further 30 minutes, stirring occasionally, until the onions are very tender.

Remove the saucepan lid and continue to cook, stirring, for another 5–10 minutes, until the onions begin to caramelise and become an even golden brown.

Add the stock and bay leaf, then simmer for another 30 minutes.

Meanwhile, preheat the oven to 160°C/320°F (fan-forced). To make the croutons, lightly brush both sides of each slice of bread with olive oil and place on a baking tray. Bake for 10 minutes on each side, until crunchy and deep golden brown.

Increase the oven temperature to 200°C/400°F (fan forced).

Remove the bay leaf from the soup. Stir in the Cognac, then taste and season with sea salt flakes and freshly ground black pepper.

Pour a small ladle of soup into six ovenproof soup bowls. Add a crouton and a sprinkling of gruyère. Ladle in the remaining soup, then add another crouton to each bowl and a thick layer of cheese.

Place the bowls on a baking tray and carefully transfer to the oven. Bake for about 5 minutes, or until the soup is bubbling hot and the cheese has formed a golden crust.

Allow to stand for a few minutes before serving, as the soup and bowls will be extremely hot.

FRAGRANT FISH SOUP WITH PAPPARDELLE

SERVES 4

200 g (7 oz) pappardelle pasta
1 tablespoon butter
200 g (7 oz) skinless firm white fish fillet, such
   as snapper, cut into 2 cm (¾ inch) pieces
12 mussels, cleaned
12 scallops
15 g (½ oz/½ cup) finely chopped flat-leaf
   (Italian) parsley
crusty bread, to serve

STOCK

2 tablespoons olive oil
2 leeks, white and pale green parts only,
   chopped
2 carrots, chopped
2 garlic cloves, bruised with the back of a knife
1 fennel bulb, sliced
2 bay leaves
3 thyme sprigs
1 teaspoon sea salt flakes
1 strip of orange zest
3 tomatoes, chopped
1.5 kg (3 lb 5 oz) heads and bones of white fish
   such as cod, flathead, perch, bream, whiting
   or snapper (see note), gills removed, cleaned
   and rinsed
60 ml (2 fl oz/¼ cup) apple cider vinegar, or
   250 ml (8½ fl oz/1 cup) dry white wine

First, prepare the stock. Heat a large heavy-based saucepan over medium heat. Add the olive oil, leek, carrot, garlic, fennel, bay leaves, thyme, salt and orange zest. Cook for 10 minutes, or until softened, stirring occasionally. Add the tomatoes, as well as the fish heads and bones. Cook, stirring occasionally, for a further 15 minutes. Pour in the vinegar or wine and 750 ml (25½ fl oz/3 cups) water. Heat until simmering, then reduce the heat and cook at a gentle simmer for a further 40 minutes.

Pour the stock through a fine sieve into a large clean saucepan, pressing out as much liquid as you can. Return the stock to a medium-low heat, adjust the seasoning and leave to simmer.

Bring a large saucepan of salted water to the boil. Add the pasta and cook until al dente. Drain, return to the pan, stir the butter through and cover to keep warm.

Add the fish fillet to the hot stock and cook for 2 minutes. Add the mussels and cook for 2 minutes more. Add the scallops, remove the soup from the heat and stir in half the parsley.

Divide the pasta among four soup bowls, then ladle the soup over. Scatter with the remaining parsley and serve with crusty bread.

X For best results, avoid using oily fish such as salmon, mackerel and ocean trout in this dish.

CHUNKY BEETROOT
& VEGETABLE SOUP

SERVES 4

2 tablespoons olive oil

1 leek, white part only, thinly sliced

2 beetroot (beets), peeled and diced

1 parsnip, peeled and diced

2 carrots, unpeeled, diced

2 bay leaves

4 garlic cloves, thinly sliced

2 teaspoons caraway seeds

100 g (3½ oz/½ cup) cracked farro (see note)
   or pearl barley

1 litre (34 fl oz/4 cups) vegetable or chicken
   stock

150 g (5½ oz/2 cups) finely shredded white
   or red cabbage

sour cream, to serve

dill sprigs, to garnish

Heat the olive oil in a large heavy-based saucepan over medium–low heat. Sauté the leek, beetroot, parsnip, carrot, bay leaves, garlic and caraway seeds for 10 minutes, or until the vegetables start to soften, stirring occasionally.

Add the farro and stock. Bring to the boil over high heat, then reduce the heat to low. Cover and simmer for 30 minutes, or until the farro is nearly tender.

Add the cabbage and a little extra water, if necessary. Cover and simmer for a further 10 minutes, or until the vegetables and farro are tender. Season to taste with sea salt flakes and freshly ground black pepper.

Serve with a dollop of sour cream, garnished with dill.

✗ Farro is an ancient, highly nutritious wheat grain that has fed the people of the Middle East and the Mediterranean for thousands of years. Cracked farro will cook more quickly than whole grains; if you only have whole farro grains, soak them overnight for quicker cooking.

SMOKY WHITE BEAN & HAM HOCK SOUP WITH GREMOLATA

SERVES 6

1 tablespoon olive oil
1 onion, finely chopped
1 carrot, halved lengthways and chopped
3 garlic cloves, crushed
500 g (1 lb 2 oz) smoked ham hock
200 g (7 oz/1 cup) dried cannellini beans, rinsed
2 litres (68 fl oz/8 cups) vegetable stock
2 teaspoons sweet paprika
2 teaspoons smoked paprika
crusty bread, to serve

GREMOLATA

zest of 1 lemon
1 long red chilli, finely chopped
15 g (½ oz/½ cup) finely chopped flat-leaf
   (Italian) parsley

Heat the olive oil in a large heavy-based saucepan over medium heat. Add the onion and carrot and cook, stirring, for 5–6 minutes, or until softened. Add the garlic and cook, stirring, for 1 minute.

Add the ham hock, beans, stock and all the paprika. Bring to the boil, then reduce the heat to low. Cover and simmer, stirring occasionally, for 2½ hours, or until the beans and hock are tender.

Remove the hock from the soup, allow to cool slightly then remove and shred the meat. Discard the skin and bone.

Transfer about one-third of the beans and carrots from the soup into a bowl. Mash roughly with a fork then stir back into the soup along with the shredded meat from the hock. Taste and season with sea salt flakes and freshly ground black pepper if required.

To make the gremolata, combine the ingredients in a small bowl.

Serve the soup in large bowls, with a sprinkle of gremolata and slices of crusty bread.

ETHIOPIAN-STYLE LENTIL & TOMATO SOUP

SERVES 6

2 tablespoons olive oil
1 brown onion, finely chopped
2 carrots, diced
3 celery stalks, halved lengthways and chopped
2 garlic cloves, crushed
400 g (14 oz) tinned crushed tomatoes
185 g (6½ oz/1 cup) brown lentils, or 250 g
  (9 oz/1 cup) red lentils, rinsed
2 litres (68 fl oz/8 cups) vegetable stock
1 potato, diced
2 tablespoons lemon juice

BERBERE SPICE MIX

⅛ teaspoon ground cloves
⅛ teaspoon ground allspice
¼ teaspoon ground nutmeg
½ teaspoon ground coriander
½ teaspoon ground fenugreek
½ teaspoon freshly ground black pepper
1 teaspoon ground cinnamon
1 teaspoon ground cardamom
1 teaspoon ground ginger
2 teaspoons chilli flakes
1 tablespoon cayenne pepper
2 tablespoons hot paprika
1 tablespoon sweet paprika

ZESTY YOGHURT TOPPING

90 g (3 oz/⅓ cup) plain yoghurt
3 tablespoons finely chopped flat-leaf
  (Italian) parsley
zest of ½ lemon

To make the Berbere spice mix, combine the ingredients in a small bowl, mixing well. Set aside in a small airtight container.

Heat the olive oil in a large saucepan over medium heat. Add the onion, carrot and celery. Cover and cook for 10 minutes, stirring occasionally, until softened but not browned. If the vegetables begin to stick to the pan and brown before they are softened, add a tablespoon of water.

Add the garlic and 2 tablespoons of the spice mix and cook, stirring, for a further minute, or until fragrant.

Stir in the tomatoes, lentils and stock. Bring to a simmer, then cover and reduce the heat to low. Simmer for 30–40 minutes, or until the lentils are tender.

Add the potato and cook for a further 10 minutes. Stir in the lemon juice.

For the yoghurt topping, combine the ingredients in a small bowl.

Serve the soup in individual bowls, with a spoonful of the zesty yoghurt on top.

X The Berbere spice mix makes more than you need for this recipe, but is useful to have on hand as a ready-made seasoning for other dishes. Store the remainder in an airtight container in the fridge and use in your next batch of soup, or to season roast chicken, steak or vegetables. It is best used within 3 months.

TUSCAN CHICKEN SOUP

SERVES 6

6 skinless chicken thighs, bone in
olive oil, for brushing and pan-frying
1 brown onion, finely diced
2 carrots, finely diced
3 celery stalks, finely diced
2 garlic cloves, crushed
2 zucchini (courgettes), diced
2 tablespoons chopped rosemary
400 g (14 oz) tinned crushed tomatoes
1 litre (34 fl oz/4 cups) chicken stock
2 teaspoons finely chopped fresh oregano,
    or 1 teaspoon dried
2 teaspoons finely chopped fresh basil,
    or 1 teaspoon dried
45 g (1½ oz/½ cup) small pasta shells
grated Pecorino Romano or parmesan cheese,
    to serve

Preheat the oven to 160°C/320°F (fan-forced). Line a baking tray with baking paper.

Brush the chicken thighs with olive oil and sprinkle with sea salt flakes and freshly ground black pepper. Place on the lined baking tray and bake for 25 minutes. Remove from the oven and rest for 10 minutes.

Meanwhile, heat a little olive oil in a large saucepan over medium heat and sauté the onion, carrot and celery for 10 minutes. Add the garlic, zucchini and rosemary and cook for a further 5 minutes.

Stir in the tomatoes, stock, oregano and basil, then simmer over low heat for 40 minutes.

Bring 2 litres (68 fl oz/8 cups) salted water to the boil in a saucepan over high heat. Cook the pasta shells until almost al dente, then drain.

Remove the chicken meat from the bones and cut into 2 cm (¾ inch) pieces. Add the pasta, chicken meat and any juices from the baking tray to the soup and simmer for a final 5 minutes.

Serve in deep bowls, scattered with the grated cheese.

CLAM CHOWDER

SERVES 4–6

2 kg (4 lb 6 oz) fresh clams, scrubbed clean
125 ml (4 fl oz/½ cup) dry white wine
150 g (5½ oz) kaiserfleisch or thick cut bacon,
    cut into 1 cm (½ inch) cubes
1 tablespoon butter
1 leek, white part only, cut in half lengthways,
    then sliced
2 celery stalks, chopped
1 bay leaf
750 ml (25½ fl oz/3 cups) full-cream milk
2 russet or other floury potatoes, peeled and
    cut into 2 cm (¾ inch) cubes
185 ml (6½ fl oz/¾ cup) pouring (single/light)
    cream
15 g (½ oz/½ cup) finely chopped flat-leaf
    (Italian) parsley

Place the clams in a large saucepan. Pour in the wine and 250 ml (8½ fl oz/1 cup) water. Cover and cook over medium heat for about 10 minutes, or until the clams have opened.

Line a sieve with muslin (cheesecloth) or paper towel and set it over a bowl. Strain the clam broth through the sieve to remove any sand or grit from the clams; reserve the cooking broth in the bowl.

When cool enough to handle, remove the clams from the shells. Discard the shells, and roughly chop any large clams. Set the clams and the broth aside separately.

Place the kaiserfleisch and 125 ml (4 fl oz/½ cup) water in a large heavy-based saucepan over medium heat. Cook, stirring occasionally, for about 10 minutes, until the water has evaporated, the pork fat rendered and the meat has begun to crisp. Remove the bacon using a slotted spoon and add to the reserved clams.

Add the butter, leek, celery and bay leaf to the pan and cook, stirring, for 8 minutes, or until the leek has softened.

Add the reserved clam broth and the milk and potatoes. Season with sea salt flakes and freshly ground black pepper and simmer gently for 15 minutes, or until the potato is cooked and starting to break down.

Transfer 500 ml (17 fl oz/2 cups) of the liquid, along with about 115 g (4 oz/½ cup) of the cooked vegetables, from the soup to a bowl. Cool slightly, then use a stick mixer to blend until smooth.

Return the blended liquid to the soup. Stir in the cream, half of the parsley and the reserved bacon and clams. Adjust the seasoning and gently reheat until simmering.

Serve in deep soup bowls, sprinkled with the remaining parsley.

MUSHROOM & BARLEY SOUP

SERVES 4

1 tablespoon olive oil

1 leek, white part only, thinly sliced

300 g (10½ oz) small portobello or Swiss
   brown mushrooms, thinly sliced

2 garlic cloves, crushed

2 tablespoons tomato paste (concentrated
   purée)

4 thyme sprigs

6 flat-leaf (Italian) parsley stalks

2 carrots, diced

2 celery stalks, sliced

200 g (7 oz/1 cup) pearl barley, rinsed

1.25 litres (42 fl oz/5 cups) chicken stock

crusty bread, to serve

Heat the olive oil in a large heavy-based saucepan over medium
heat. Add the leek and cook, covered, stirring occasionally, for
5 minutes, or until starting to soften.

Add the mushrooms. Cover the pan and cook, stirring occasionally,
for 5 minutes, or until they start to release their juices. Add the garlic
and tomato paste and cook, stirring, for a further minute.

Tie the thyme and parsley together with kitchen string. Add to the
pan with the carrot, celery, barley and stock. Cover and bring to
the boil, then reduce the heat to low. Simmer, partially covered, for
35–40 minutes, or until the barley is tender.

Add a little boiling water to adjust the consistency to your liking.
Season to taste with sea salt flakes and freshly ground black pepper.

Remove the herb bundle, stripping the thyme leaves from the stalks
and stirring them into the soup. Serve with crusty bread.

✕ Soaking the barley overnight in water will reduce the
   cooking time.

BORLOTTI BEAN & BACON SOUP WITH BASIL OIL

SERVES 4

250 g (9 oz/1¼ cups) dried borlotti
    (cranberry) beans
100 g (3½ oz) diced bacon
2 tablespoons olive oil
1 large onion, finely chopped
2 carrots, chopped
2 celery stalks, chopped
3 garlic cloves, finely chopped
2 rosemary sprigs
2 bay leaves
1 tablespoon tomato paste (concentrated purée)
2 potatoes, peeled and chopped
1 litre (34 fl oz/4 cups) vegetable stock
crusty bread, to serve

BASIL OIL

25 g (1 oz/½ cup, firmly packed) basil leaves
1 small garlic clove, peeled
60 ml (2 fl oz/¼ cup) olive oil

Put the beans in a large bowl, cover with plenty of cold water and soak overnight. Drain and set aside.

Fry the bacon in a large saucepan over high heat for 2–3 minutes, until lightly browned. Add the olive oil, onion, carrot and celery and cook over medium heat for 5 minutes, or until the vegetables are lightly browned and just softened. Add the garlic, rosemary, bay leaves and tomato paste and cook, stirring, for 1–2 minutes.

Add the drained beans along with the potatoes, stock and 1 litre (34 fl oz/4 cups) water. Partially cover and bring to a simmer. Cook, partially covered, over low heat for 1 hour, removing any scum that rises to the surface. Allow to cool slightly.

Remove the bay leaves and strip the rosemary sprigs, discarding the stems and returning the leaves to the soup. Season to taste with sea salt flakes and freshly ground black pepper.

Combine the basil oil ingredients in a small food processor with a small pinch of salt. Blend to a smooth purée.

Blend the soup roughly using a stick blender, or, in two batches, transfer to a food processor and blend until just smooth, with some vegetables and beans still remaining quite whole.

Gently reheat the soup. Ladle into bowls, drizzle with the basil oil and serve with crusty bread.

X If you prefer a slightly thicker soup, increase the potato to 400 g (14 oz), or add a small handful of short pasta (such as ditalini) at the same time as the beans and simmer it in the soup.

CARIBBEAN-STYLE BLACK BEAN SOUP

SERVES 4

220 g (8 oz/1 cup) dried black beans
1 tablespoon olive oil
2 celery stalks, chopped
2 carrots, chopped
1 leek, white part only, finely sliced
3 garlic cloves, crushed
1 jalapeño chilli, seeded and finely chopped
1 teaspoon smoked paprika
½ teaspoon ground allspice
60 g (2 oz/¼ cup) tomato paste
    (concentrated purée)
400 g (14 oz) tinned crushed tomatoes
1 orange sweet potato, peeled and diced
large handful of coriander (cilantro) leaves
    and stalks, chopped
sour cream or plain yogurt, to serve
1 lime, cut into wedges
cornbread, to serve

Put the beans in a large bowl, cover with plenty of cold water and soak overnight. Drain and set aside.

Heat the olive oil in a large heavy-based saucepan over medium heat. Sauté the celery, carrot and leek, stirring occasionally, for 10–12 minutes, or until softened. Add the garlic, jalapeño chilli and spices and cook, stirring, until fragrant. Stir in the tomato paste and cook for 2 minutes.

Add the beans and 1 litre (34 fl oz/4 cups) water. Increase the heat to high and bring to the boil, then reduce the heat to medium. Simmer, partially covered, for 1¼ hours, stirring occasionally, and adding a little more water if the mixture starts to dry out.

Add the tomatoes and sweet potato and simmer for a further 30 minutes, or until the beans are soft.

Season to taste with sea salt flakes and freshly ground black pepper, then stir in the coriander.

Serve with sour cream, lime wedges and cornbread.

VEGETABLES

STUFFED POBLANOS

SERVES 4

4 large poblano chillies (see note)
75 g (2½ oz/½ cup) grated mozzarella

FILLING

100 g (3½ oz/½ cup) quinoa, rinsed
3 corn cobs, kernels removed
400 g (14 oz) tinned black beans,
    rinsed and drained
150 g (5½ oz/1 cup) crumbled feta
25 g (1 oz/½ cup) chopped coriander
    (cilantro) leaves
1 teaspoon ground cumin
juice of 1 lime

SAUCE

2 tablespoons olive oil
1 small onion, finely chopped
1 small sweet potato, grated
2 garlic cloves, crushed
1 jalapeño chilli, seeds removed,
    finely chopped
700 ml (23½ fl oz) tomato passata
1 teaspoon sea salt flakes
¼ teaspoon dried oregano

Preheat the oven to 150°C/300°F (fan-forced). Lightly grease a 20 cm × 30 cm (8 inch × 12 inch) baking dish.

To make the sauce, heat the olive oil in a saucepan over medium heat and sauté the onion and sweet potato for about 5 minutes, stirring occasionally. Add the garlic and jalapeño chilli and cook for a further 2 minutes. Add the passata, salt and oregano and simmer over low heat for 10 minutes.

Meanwhile, start preparing the filling. In a small saucepan, bring the quinoa and 250 ml (8½ fl oz/1 cup) water to the boil over medium heat. Reduce the heat to low, then cover and simmer for 15 minutes. Drain off any excess liquid and place in a large mixing bowl with the corn, beans, feta and coriander. Sprinkle the cumin and lime juice over and mix together well.

Leaving the stems intact, cut the poblano chillies in half lengthways, removing the ribs and seeds. Evenly divide the filling mixture among the poblano halves.

Pour the tomato sauce mixture into the baking dish. Add the poblano halves, placing them in the baking dish, filling side up.

Place a sheet of baking paper over the dish, then cover tightly with foil. Transfer to the oven and bake for 1 hour.

Remove the foil and baking paper. Sprinkle the mozzarella over the poblano halves and bake for a further 20 minutes, or until the cheese has melted. Allow to cool a little before serving.

✕ If you can't find poblano chillies, use small red capsicums (bell peppers) instead.

PUMPKIN, SILVERBEET & TOFU CURRY

SERVES 4

2 tablespoons peanut oil
200 g (7 oz) firm tofu, cut into 2 cm (¾ inch) cubes
1 teaspoon black mustard seeds
½ teaspoon ground turmeric
500 g (1 lb 2 oz) silverbeet (Swiss chard), stalks thinly sliced, leaves shredded
2 garlic cloves, crushed
3 cm (1¼ inch) piece of fresh ginger, peeled and finely grated
1 tablespoon curry powder
500 g (1 lb 2 oz) pumpkin (winter squash), peeled, seeded and cut into 4 cm (1½ inch) pieces
2 carrots, cut into strips
500 ml (17 fl oz/2 cups) vegetable stock
200 g (7 oz) cauliflower, cut into florets
100 g (3½ oz) snow peas (mangetout), trimmed
185 ml (6½ fl oz/¾ cup) coconut milk
steamed white rice, to serve
handful of coriander (cilantro) sprigs, to garnish

Heat half the peanut oil in a large heavy-based saucepan over medium heat. Add the tofu, mustard seeds and turmeric and gently stir-fry for 1–2 minutes, or until the tofu is well coated and lightly browned. Remove the tofu from the pan and set aside.

Add the remaining oil to the pan, along with the silverbeet stalks. Stir, then cover and cook over medium–low heat for 3–5 minutes, or until just tender, stirring occasionally. Add the garlic, ginger and curry powder and cook, stirring, for another 1–2 minutes, or until fragrant.

Now add the pumpkin, carrot and stock. Bring to a simmer, then cover and leave to cook for 10 minutes.

Stir in the cauliflower and silverbeet leaves, cover and cook for 6 minutes.

Return the tofu to the pan, stir gently, and add the snow peas and coconut milk. Cook, uncovered, for a final 5 minutes, or until the tofu is heated through and the cauliflower is tender. As the pumpkin cooks it will start to break down a little, thickening the sauce slightly.

Serve with steamed rice, scattered with coriander.

SLOW-COOKED BAKED BEANS

SERVES 4

400 g (14 oz/2 cups) dried haricot, cannellini
  or borlotti (cranberry) beans
2 tablespoons salt
60 ml (2 fl oz/¼ cup) extra virgin olive oil
2 red onions, finely chopped
2 garlic cloves, finely chopped
1 carrot, chopped
2 celery stalks, diced
1 bay leaf
2 teaspoons sweet paprika
400 g (14 oz) tinned crushed tomatoes
185 ml (6½ fl oz/¾ cup) tomato passata
1½ teaspoons sea salt flakes
2 tablespoons dark muscovado sugar
60 ml (2 fl oz/¼ cup) cider vinegar
fried eggs, sourdough toast and/or salad,
  to serve (optional)

Put the beans in a large bowl and sprinkle with the salt. Cover with plenty of cold water and leave to soak for 8 hours, or overnight.

The next day, preheat the oven to 140°C/275°F (fan-forced).

Drain the beans, place in a saucepan and cover with cold water. Bring to the boil, then reduce the heat and simmer for 10 minutes. Drain, rinse with cold water and set aside.

Heat the olive oil in a large flameproof casserole dish over medium heat. Add the onion, garlic, carrot and celery and cook, stirring, for 10 minutes. Add the drained beans, bay leaf and paprika, and mix.

Stir in the tomatoes, passata, salt flakes, sugar and vinegar. Add 2 litres (68 fl oz/8 cups) water, or enough to generously cover the beans by 10 cm (4 inches).

Bring the mixture to a gentle boil, then cover the pan with a sheet of baking paper. Put the lid on and carefully transfer to the oven. Bake for 2 hours.

Check the beans and give the mixture a stir. The sauce should be a little runny, but starting to thicken; if it looks dry, add a little water. Return to the oven and bake for a further 1 hour, or until the beans are tender, in a rich, thick, glossy sauce.

Serve for breakfast, lunch or dinner, with eggs on sourdough toast, or with salad.

ROASTED PUMPKIN RISOTTO WITH BROWNED BUTTER, SAGE, ORANGE & PINE NUTS

SERVES 4

600 g (1 lb 5 oz) butternut or kent pumpkin
(winter squash), peeled and cut into 2 cm
(¾ inch) chunks
2½ tablespoons olive oil
1.25 litres (42 fl oz/5 cups) vegetable or
chicken stock
75 g (2½ oz) butter
1 onion, finely chopped
2 large garlic cloves, finely chopped
1 bay leaf
2 thyme sprigs
330 g (11½ oz/1½ cups) arborio rice
125 ml (4 fl oz/½ cup) dry white wine
large handful of baby English spinach leaves
40 g (1½ oz/¼ cup) pine nuts or crushed walnuts
small handful of sage leaves
2 teaspoons orange zest
finely grated parmesan, to serve

Preheat the oven to 170°C/340°F (fan-forced). Line a baking tray with baking paper.

Put the pumpkin in a large bowl. Drizzle with 1½ tablespoons of the olive oil, sprinkle generously with sea salt flakes and freshly ground black pepper and toss to combine. Place on the lined baking tray and roast for 30 minutes, or until golden.

Pour the stock into a saucepan and bring just to the boil. Turn off the heat.

In a large shallow saucepan or deep frying pan, heat the remaining olive oil and a third of the butter. Cook the onion over low heat for 5 minutes, or until softened. Add the garlic, bay leaf, thyme sprigs and rice, stirring to coat the rice in the oil.

Stir in the wine. Gradually add the hot stock, a ladleful at a time, stirring until the stock has been almost absorbed. Keep adding the stock gradually, cooking over low heat.

Stir in the pumpkin with the last addition of stock, mashing it lightly as you stir. Remove the bay leaf and thyme sprigs, discarding the bay leaf, and stripping the leaves off the thyme and adding them back into the risotto. Stir the spinach through.

Melt the remaining butter in a separate frying pan over medium heat. Allow it to foam, then add the pine nuts and sage, swirling the pan as the butter and nuts become golden and start to smell nutty, and the sage becomes a little crispy. Add the orange zest, swirling to heat it through, then immediately pour the butter mixture over the risotto.

Season to taste and serve sprinkled with plenty of grated parmesan.

BAKED EGGPLANT PARMIGIANA

SERVES 4–6

1.5 kg (3 lb 5 oz) eggplants (aubergines),
    sliced 5 mm (¼ inch) thick
125 ml (4 fl oz/½ cup) olive oil, plus extra
    for the topping
75 g (2½ oz/½ cup) grated mozzarella
15 g (½ oz/¼ cup) panko breadcrumbs
25 g (1 oz/¼ cup) finely grated parmesan
fresh basil leaves, to garnish (optional)

SUGO

2 tablespoons olive oil
1 red onion, finely chopped
2 garlic cloves, crushed
¼ teaspoon chilli flakes
400 g (14 oz) tinned crushed tomatoes
500 ml (17 fl oz/2 cups) tomato passata
2 teaspoons balsamic vinegar
1 teaspoon sea salt flakes
2 basil sprigs

To make the sugo, heat the olive oil in a saucepan over medium-low heat. Add the onion and cook gently for 10 minutes, stirring occasionally, and adding a little water if it starts to brown. Add the garlic and chilli flakes and cook for a minute further. Stir in the tomatoes, passata, vinegar, salt, basil and 125 ml (4 fl oz/ ½ cup) water. Bring to a low boil, then cover and simmer over low heat for 15 minutes, or until the mixture has reduced and thickened to a saucy consistency.

Meanwhile, preheat the oven to 150°C/300°F (fan-forced). Lightly grease a 20 cm (8 inch) baking dish.

Heat a large heavy-based frying pan over medium-high heat. Brush some of the eggplant slices with some of the olive oil and cook on each side for 1 minute, or until golden brown. Remove to a plate lined with paper towel and finish cooking the remaining eggplant slices.

Lay some of the eggplant slices in the baking dish, in a single layer. Spread a cupful of the sugo over the top. Repeat with more eggplant and sugo layers, finishing with the sugo. Scatter the mozzarella over the top. Cover the dish with foil, transfer to the oven and bake for 1 hour.

Remove the dish from the oven and remove the foil. To make a topping, toss the breadcrumbs with a good drizzle of olive oil in a small bowl, scatter evenly over the bake, then sprinkle with the parmesan. Bake for a further 30 minutes, or until the topping is crunchy and golden.

Remove from the oven and allow to stand for 5 minutes. If you like, serve scattered with basil leaves.

✕ For this recipe, choose fresh glossy small eggplants, as they will not need salting to draw out any bitter juices.

SRI LANKAN DHAL CURRY

SERVES 4

400 g (14 oz) red lentils, well rinsed
1 cinnamon stick
3 garlic cloves, crushed
1½ teaspoons ground turmeric
½ teaspoon sea salt flakes
80 ml (2½ fl oz/⅓ cup) coconut milk
coriander (cilantro) leaves, to garnish
steamed white rice or warm roti, to serve

SPICE OIL

2 tablespoons peanut oil
½ teaspoon black mustard seeds
½ teaspoon cumin seeds
½ teaspoon fenugreek seeds
1 onion, thinly sliced
small handful of fresh curry leaves
1–2 long green chillies, thinly sliced
1 tomato, chopped

Place the lentils in a heavy-based saucepan with the cinnamon stick, garlic, turmeric and salt. Add 1 litre (34 fl oz/4 cups) water and bring to the boil over medium heat. Reduce the heat to low and simmer, stirring occasionally, for 20–25 minutes, until the lentils are almost tender; add a little more water if the mixture starts to stick.

Stir in the coconut milk and return to a simmer. Cook for a further 5–10 minutes, until the lentils are tender. Remove from the heat and cover to keep warm.

To prepare the spice oil, heat the peanut oil in a heavy-based frying pan over medium heat. Add the mustard seeds and, when they start to pop, add the cumin and fenugreek seeds. Cook for a further 30 seconds, then add the onion, curry leaves and chilli. Cook, stirring, for 2–3 minutes, or until the onion has softened slightly. Add the tomato and cook for a further 2 minutes, or until the tomato has just softened.

Pour the dhal into a serving dish. Drizzle with the spice oil, garnish with coriander and serve with rice or roti.

ROAST PORTOBELLO MUSHROOMS WITH BLUE CHEESE & PINE NUT STUFFING

SERVES 4

8 medium-sized portobello mushrooms
40 g (1½ oz) butter
2 French shallots, finely diced
2 garlic cloves, crushed
1 generous teaspoon picked thyme leaves
80 g (2¾ oz/1 cup) fresh breadcrumbs
200 g (7 oz) stilton, crumbled
40 g (1½ oz/¼ cup) pine nuts, toasted
1 tablespoon olive oil
baby red sorrel leaves, to garnish (optional)

CHARRED RED CAPSICUM SAUCE

2 red capsicums (bell peppers)
150 g (5½ oz) sour cream
1 teaspoon lemon juice
1 garlic clove, crushed

To make the sauce, place the capsicums on a heated barbecue, or directly on a gas burner over medium heat, and cook for 7–10 minutes, rotating regularly with tongs, until blackened all over. Transfer to a zip-lock bag and place in the freezer. Once cooled, gently remove the skin, stems and seeds. Place the capsicum flesh into the small bowl of a food processor, along with the sour cream, lemon juice and garlic. Blend until combined into a smooth sauce. Set aside.

Preheat the oven to 170°C/340°F (fan-forced). Line a baking tray with baking paper.

Remove the stalks from the mushrooms. Trim and discard the woody ends, then finely chop the stalks.

Melt the butter in a frying pan over medium heat and sauté the shallot, garlic and chopped mushroom stalks for 5–7 minutes, until softened. Stir the thyme through, transfer to a bowl and leave to cool slightly.

Add the breadcrumbs, stilton and pine nuts to the shallot mixture and mix to combine.

Brush the outside of the mushrooms with the olive oil. Divide the stuffing between the mushrooms, patting it down firmly to keep it in place.

Transfer the stuffed mushrooms to the baking tray and roast for 15 minutes.

Serve warm, with the roasted capsicum sauce, garnished with baby red sorrel leaves if desired.

ROASTED EGGPLANT WITH TAHINI SAUCE & POMEGRANATE

Using a sharp knife, cut each eggplant in half lengthways, then score the cut side of each half in a diamond pattern. Season generously with salt, and leave to sit for 30 minutes.

Meanwhile, grind the cumin seeds using a mortar and pestle, mix with the olive oil and set aside.

Preheat the oven to 180°C/350°F (fan-forced).

Rinse the salted eggplant thoroughly with water, then pat dry with paper towel. Brush each cut side with the cumin and oil mixture, then place on a baking tray, cut side up.

Transfer to the oven and roast for 20 minutes, or until the flesh is tender.

While the eggplant is roasting, combine all the tahini sauce ingredients in a small bowl, mixing well. Season to taste with salt and freshly ground black pepper and set aside.

To remove the seeds from the pomegranate, cut the fruit in half. Hold one half, cut side down, in the palm of your hand with your fingers spread, over a wide bowl. Use the back of a ladle or a rolling pin to firmly tap the skin of the pomegranate – the seeds should fall out into the bowl. Once it looks like all the seeds have been released, pick through the bowl to remove any white bits of the pith that have fallen in.

Place the roasted eggplant on a platter and drizzle evenly with the tahini sauce. Scatter over the parsley and pomegranate seeds and serve.

SERVES 4

4 medium-sized eggplants (aubergines)
1 teaspoon cumin seeds
2 tablespoons olive oil
1 pomegranate
2 tablespoons chopped parsley

TAHINI SAUCE

1 tablespoon tahini
250 g (9 oz/1 cup) Greek-style yoghurt
1 garlic clove, crushed
½ teaspoon pomegranate molasses
zest and juice of ½ lemon

MUSHROOM & WINTER VEGETABLE WELLINGTON

SERVES 6–8

20 g (¾ oz) dried porcini mushrooms

30 g (1 oz) butter

1 onion, finely chopped

3 garlic cloves, finely chopped

1 celery stalk, finely diced

1 carrot, finely diced

1 leek, white part only, sliced

2 teaspoons chopped thyme

100 g (3½ oz) chestnuts, finely chopped;
   tinned or vacuum-packed are fine

300 g (10½ oz) mixed fresh mushrooms, such
   as field, cup and shiitake, roughly chopped

1 tablespoon olive oil

8 sage leaves, chopped

2 tablespoons Pedro Ximénez, or any
   good-quality sweet sherry

70 g (2½ oz) fresh breadcrumbs

zest of 1 lemon

large handful chopped parsley

300 g (10½ oz) kale, coarse stems removed,
   leaves chopped

Place the dried porcini in a small bowl, cover with 125 ml (4 fl oz/ ½ cup) hot water and set aside to soak.

Melt the butter in a large saucepan over medium heat and add the onion, garlic, celery, carrot and leek. Give everything a good stir until the vegetables are well coated in the butter, then stir through the thyme. Season well with salt and freshly ground black pepper.

Reduce the heat to medium–low, partially cover with a lid and cook, stirring occasionally, for about 20 minutes, or until the vegetables are completely soft. Stir the chestnuts through, check and adjust the seasoning if necessary, then set aside to cool.

Preheat the oven to 180°C/350°F (fan-forced). Line a large baking tray with foil.

Blitz the fresh mushrooms in a food processor and set aside. Strain the porcini mushrooms, reserving the liquid, and finely chop.

Heat the olive oil in a large frying pan over medium heat and add the porcini and sage. Cook for 2–3 minutes, stirring regularly, then increase the heat to medium–high. Add the chopped fresh mushrooms from the food processor, season well and cook, stirring frequently, until the mixture has reduced and is starting to brown.

Deglaze the pan with the sherry, stirring until the liquid is absorbed. Pour in the reserved porcini soaking liquid and reduce the heat to medium. Cook, stirring frequently, until the liquid is completely absorbed.

Transfer the mushroom mixture to a large bowl. Add the sautéed vegetables, then stir through the breadcrumbs, lemon zest and parsley. Check the seasoning and adjust if necessary.

Steam the kale for 3–4 minutes, or until wilted. Drain well and set aside.

plain (all-purpose) flour, for dusting
350 g (12½ oz) block of frozen puff pastry, thawed
100 g (3½ oz) stilton
1 free-range egg, whisked with 1 tablespoon milk

MUSHROOM GRAVY
50 g (1¾ oz) butter
250 g (9 oz) mushrooms, such as field and cup mushrooms, finely sliced
4 French shallots, finely chopped
4 thyme sprigs
35 g (1¼ oz/¼ cup) plain (all-purpose) flour
750 ml (25½ fl oz/3 cups) vegetable stock
1 tablespoon soy sauce

On a lightly floured work surface, roll out the puff pastry to a large rectangle, about 5 mm (¼ inch) thick. Squeeze as much liquid as possible from the steamed kale and scatter it over the pastry, leaving a 2 cm (¾ inch) border around the edges. Spoon the vegetable mixture onto the long side of the pastry nearest to you, then form into a large log – it will look huge! Break the stilton into small chunks and dot over the vegetables.

Brush the edges of the pastry with the egg wash, then gently lift the side that's nearest to you and roll the pastry into a large sausage roll — the two long edges should overlap by about 4 cm (1½ inches).

Transfer to the lined baking tray, seam side down, and close the short ends of the wellington by pinching and pleating the pastry.

Brush the pastry with the egg wash, then cut some slits in the top using a sharp knife, to let the steam escape.

Bake for 30–40 minutes, or until the pastry is browned and crisp. Remove from the oven and let the pastry settle for a minute or two before carving.

While the wellington is still in the oven, make the mushroom gravy. Melt the butter in a saucepan over medium heat. Add the mushroom, shallot and thyme, increase the heat to medium–high and cook, stirring frequently, for about 8 minutes, or until slightly browned. Add the flour and cook, stirring, for 2–3 minutes, or until the flour looks lightly toasted. Add the stock 250 ml (8½ fl oz/1 cup) at a time, stirring constantly until the sauce has thickened after each addition. Add the soy sauce and season with salt and freshly ground black pepper. Cook for a further minute.

Cut the wellington into thick slices and serve with the mushroom gravy poured over the top.

MUSHROOM & WINTER VEGETABLE WELLINGTON
✕

ROASTED
ROOT VEGIES

SERVES 6

2 rosemary sprigs, leaves picked
small handful thyme, leaves picked
90 ml (3 fl oz/⅓ cup) olive oil
2 large beetroot (beets), peeled and
    cut into chunks
6 baby carrots, scrubbed
3 parsnips, peeled and cut in half
250 g (9 oz) celeriac, peeled and cut
    into chunks
1 sweet potato, cut into chunks
250 g (9 oz) pumpkin (winter squash),
    peeled and cut into chunks
20 g (¾ oz) butter
1 garlic clove, finely chopped
2 × 420 g (15 oz) tins chickpeas, drained
40 g (1½ oz/¼ cup) cashews, chopped
small handful parsley, roughly chopped
1 tablespoon sumac

BERBERE SPICE MIX

1 teaspoon cumin seeds
4 whole cloves
3 cardamom pods
½ teaspoon black peppercorns
1 teaspoon fenugreek seeds
1 teaspoon coriander seeds
4 small dried red chillies
1 teaspoon salt
½ teaspoon ground ginger
½ teaspoon ground turmeric
2 tablespoons smoked paprika
¼ teaspoon ground allspice
pinch of ground cinnamon

TAHINI SAUCE

3 tablespoons tahini
juice of 1½ lemons
1 garlic clove, finely chopped
1 teaspoon salt

To make the berbere spice mix, toast the whole spices lightly in a dry frying pan over medium heat until fragrant. Using a mortar and pestle, grind to a fine powder with all the remaining spice mix ingredients. Set aside.

Add the tahini sauce ingredients to a small screw-top jar. Pour in 60 ml (2 fl oz/¼ cup) water, seal the lid on and shake until well combined. If you would like a thinner sauce, add a little more water. Set aside.

Preheat the oven to 200°C/400°F (fan-forced).

Combine the rosemary, thyme and olive oil in a small screw-top jar and season well with salt and freshly ground black pepper.

Place the beetroot in a small roasting tin and drizzle with 1 tablespoon of the herbed oil mixture. Mix well with your hands, then roast for 50 minutes.

Place the carrots, parsnip, celeriac and sweet potato in a large roasting tin and pour over half of the remaining oil. Rub the vegetables in the oil, then transfer to the oven and roast for 20 minutes.

Add the pumpkin and remaining herbed oil to the roasting tin, stirring to combine, then roast for a further 20 minutes, or until all the vegetables are cooked through.

Meanwhile, melt the butter in a frying pan over medium heat. Add the garlic and cook, stirring, until just starting to brown. Add the chickpeas and increase the heat to medium–high. Add 2 tablespoons of the reserved berbere spice mix and cook, stirring constantly, for 4–5 minutes, or until the chickpeas are dry and starting to become crisp. Set aside.

Pile the roasted vegetables onto a serving platter and scatter with the spiced chickpeas. Drizzle with the tahini sauce, scatter with the cashews and parsley, sprinkle with the sumac and serve.

X The Berbere spice mix makes more than you need for this recipe, but is useful to have on hand as a ready-made seasoning for other dishes. Store the remainder in an airtight container in the fridge and use to season soup, roast chicken or steak. It is best used within 3 months.

COUSCOUS-STUFFED CAPSICUM

SERVES 4

4 red or yellow capsicums (bell peppers)
185 g (6½ oz/1 cup) couscous
375 ml (12½ fl oz/1½ cups) hot vegetable stock
60 ml (2 fl oz/¼ cup) olive oil
4 French shallots, finely chopped
3 garlic cloves, finely chopped
2 teaspoons ground cumin
zest of 2 lemons
large handful parsley, roughly chopped
60 g (2 oz/½ cup) slivered almonds, toasted
2 tablespoons currants
100 g (3½ oz/⅔ cup) crumbled feta
juice of 1 lemon

Preheat the oven to 160°C/320°F (fan-forced).

Using a sharp knife, slice the tops off the capsicums, then scoop out the seeds and white membrane. Blanch the capsicums in a large saucepan of boiling water for 5 minutes. Drain, then transfer to a plate, placing the capsicums upside down to drain completely.

Tip the couscous into a shallow bowl and pour the hot stock over. Leave to stand for 5 minutes, then fluff up the grains with a fork.

Heat 1 tablespoon of the olive oil in a frying pan over medium heat. Add the shallot and garlic and cook for about 10 minutes, or until light golden. Stir in the cumin and cook for a further 2 minutes. Add the lemon zest and parsley and stir well to combine. Remove from the heat and set aside.

Drizzle 1 tablespoon of the remaining olive oil over the couscous and season with salt and freshly ground black pepper. Add the shallot mixture, slivered almonds, currants, feta and lemon juice and stir well to combine.

Fill the hollow capsicums with the couscous mixture, then sit them upright in a baking dish. Drizzle with the remaining oil.

Transfer to the oven and roast for about 30 minutes, or until the couscous is lightly browned on top. Enjoy warm.

WHOLE STUFFED PUMPKIN

SERVES 8

60 ml (2 fl oz/¼ cup) olive oil

200 g (7 oz) uncracked freekeh, rinsed

1½ teaspoons coriander seeds, crushed

1½ teaspoons cumin seeds, crushed

1 litre (34 fl oz/4 cups) vegetable stock

40 g (1½ oz/⅓ cup) slivered almonds, toasted

3 large garlic cloves, finely chopped

70 g (2½ oz/½ cup) dried cranberries

2 large rosemary sprigs, leaves picked and chopped

large handful parsley, roughly chopped

1 large pumpkin (winter squash), weighing at least 2 kg (4 lb 6 oz)

60 ml (2 fl oz/¼ cup) maple syrup

60 ml (2 fl oz/¼ cup) apple cider vinegar

Heat a small splash of the olive oil in a saucepan over medium heat. Add the freekeh and coriander and cumin seeds and cook until the mixture starts to sizzle and pop. Add the stock and simmer, stirring occasionally, for 45 minutes, or up to 1 hour, until the freekeh is cooked through. Transfer to a large bowl and add the almonds, garlic, cranberries, rosemary and parsley. Mix well and season to taste.

Meanwhile, preheat the oven to 200°C/400°F (fan-forced).

Using a large kitchen knife, cut out the top of the pumpkin and set aside to use as a lid. Scoop out the seeds and fibres with a spoon and discard. If your pumpkin is very thick in places, scoop out a little of the pumpkin until it is even on all sides – this will help the pumpkin to cook evenly.

In a small bowl, combine the maple syrup, vinegar and remaining olive oil. Season with salt and freshly ground black pepper, then pour over the freekeh. Toss to combine and check the seasoning.

Spoon the freekeh into the pumpkin shell. Place the pumpkin lid on top and wrap the whole pumpkin in two layers of foil.

Place on a baking tray, transfer to the oven and roast for 1 hour. Remove the foil and roast for at least another 1 hour. The pumpkin may seem soft at this stage when tested with a sharp knife, but it takes a long time to cook all the way through. You can test it's done by inserting a knife into the middle and scraping off a little of the pumpkin flesh inside. If it is still a little fibrous, cook the pumpkin for longer.

Allow the pumpkin to rest for 10 minutes before slicing into large wedges.

HARISSA-ROASTED CAULIFLOWER WITH FIG & YOGHURT SAUCE

SERVES 4

185 g (6½ oz/¾ cup) plain yoghurt
1 whole cauliflower
25 g (1 oz/¼ cup) flaked almonds
1 tablespoon chopped parsley

HARISSA

4 long red chillies
½ teaspoon caraway seeds
½ teaspoon coriander seeds
¾ teaspoon cumin seeds
½ teaspoon smoked paprika
3 garlic cloves
½ teaspoon rock salt
½ teaspoon freshly ground black pepper
1 tablespoon olive oil
1 roasted red capsicum (bell pepper),
   from a jar (or see page 51)
juice of ½ lemon

FIG & YOGHURT SAUCE

125 g (4½ oz/½ cup) plain yoghurt
1 teaspoon tahini
zest of 1 lemon
1 small garlic clove, crushed
2 dried figs, finely chopped

Preheat the oven to 160°C/320°F (fan-forced). Line a deep-sided baking dish with foil.

To make the harissa, cut two of the chillies in half lengthways and remove the seeds and membranes. Roughly chop all four chillies and set aside. In a small frying pan, toast the caraway, coriander and cumin seeds over medium heat for a minute or two, until fragrant. Tip the toasted seeds into the small bowl of a food processor. Add the remaining harissa ingredients, including the chopped chillies, and blend until everything is chopped and you have a thickish paste.

Mix half the harissa through the 185 g (6½ oz/¾ cup) yoghurt, then taste to check if it is spicy or hot enough for you. Add more harissa to your taste, until the heat is to your liking.

Remove the core and any outer leaves from the cauliflower. Brush the harissa yoghurt mixture all over the cauliflower, ensuring it is evenly coated on all sides.

Transfer the coated cauliflower to the baking dish and into the oven. Roast for 30 minutes.

Add 125 ml (4 fl oz/½ cup) water to the dish, cover with a lid or foil, and roast the cauliflower for a further 20 minutes, or until tender.

Meanwhile, to make the fig and yoghurt sauce, mix the ingredients together in a small bowl until well combined.

Serve the cauliflower warm, with the fig and yoghurt sauce, sprinkled with the almonds and parsley.

ROASTED GARLIC
& TOMATO TART

SERVES 4

3 whole garlic bulbs, unpeeled
olive oil, for drizzling
1 sheet frozen puff pastry, thawed
milk, for brushing
200 g (7 oz) good-quality ricotta
zest of 1 lemon (optional)
300 g (10½ oz) cherry tomatoes, cut in half
small handful thyme sprigs, leaves picked
green salad, to serve
balsamic vinegar, for drizzling

Preheat the oven to 160°C/320°F (fan-forced). Line a baking tray with foil.

Slice the top one-quarter off the garlic bulbs and discard. Place the garlic bulbs on a large square of foil and drizzle with a little olive oil. Wrap the garlic in the foil and roast in the oven for 40 minutes, or until completely soft. Set aside to cool.

Trim off and reserve about 1 cm (½ inch) from each side of the pastry. Place the pastry on the lined baking tray. Brush the outer edges of the pastry with milk and place the trimmed edges on top, to form a small crust during baking.

Squeeze the roasted garlic cloves from the bulbs, into a small bowl. Add the ricotta and lemon zest, if using. Season generously with salt and freshly ground black pepper and mix well.

Spread the ricotta mixture over the pastry, avoiding the border around the edge. Arrange the tomatoes on top, cut side up. Sprinkle with the thyme, drizzle with a little more oil and season with salt and pepper.

Transfer to the oven and bake for about 30 minutes, or until the pastry is golden brown.

Serve immediately, with a fresh green salad, and balsamic vinegar to drizzle over the tart.

FISH & SEAFOOD

CONFIT SALMON WITH SHAVED FENNEL & ORANGE SALAD

SERVES 4

1 litre (34 fl oz/4 cups) light olive oil

2 bay leaves

3 strips of lemon peel

4 thyme sprigs

4 × 200 g (7 oz) skinless salmon fillets

2 baby fennel bulbs, shaved

90 g (3 oz/2 cups) baby rocket (arugula) leaves

50 g (1¾ oz/1 cup, firmly packed) baby
   English spinach leaves

2 oranges, segmented (see note)

1 lemon, segmented (see note)

pinch of sea salt flakes

2 teaspoons extra virgin olive oil

Preheat the oven to 100°C/210°F (fan-forced).

Pour the light olive oil into a 20 cm (8 inch) square baking dish. Add the bay leaves, lemon peel and thyme sprigs. Place the dish in the oven for 30 minutes, to gently warm the oil and allow the herb flavours to infuse.

Carefully place the salmon fillets into the oil. Bake for 14–15 minutes, then remove the dish from the oven.

Lift the salmon pieces onto a plate lined with paper towel, leaving the salmon to drain. Warm four plates in the residual heat of the oven.

To prepare the salad, combine the fennel, rocket, spinach and orange and lemon segments in a large bowl. Dress with the sea salt flakes and extra virgin olive oil and toss.

Place a salmon fillet on each warm plate and pile the salad on top. Serve immediately.

✕ To segment citrus, place on a chopping board and carefully cut off the top and bottom, using a sharp knife. Sit the fruit on the chopping board, so it has a flat, stable base. Working your way all around the fruit, using downward strokes and following the curved shape, cut away the peel and all the bitter white pith. Working with one citrus segment at a time, cut closely to the white membrane on each side of the segment, to release each fruit segment, reserving any juices for dressing the salad.

SALT-BAKED SNAPPER WITH SALSA VERDE

SERVES 2–3

2 kg (4 lb 6 oz) rock salt
2 free-range egg whites
½ lemon
1 teaspoon coriander seeds, lightly crushed
1–1.2 kg (2 lb 3 oz–2 lb 10 oz) whole white
     snapper, scaled and cleaned
olive oil, for drizzling
2 rosemary sprigs
3–4 thyme sprigs
crusty bread and green salad, to serve
     (optional)

SALSA VERDE

3 large anchovy fillets, finely chopped
2 garlic cloves, finely chopped
1 tablespoon baby capers, drained and rinsed
1 teaspoon dijon mustard
juice of 1 lemon
large handful parsley, finely chopped
small handful basil, finely chopped
small handful dill (optional), chopped
3–4 tablespoons olive oil

Preheat the oven to 180°C/350°F (fan-forced).

To make the salsa verde, put the anchovy and garlic in a small bowl and mash with the back of a fork. Add the capers, mustard and lots of freshly ground black pepper, and mix well. Add the lemon juice and herbs and stir well to combine. Drizzle over the olive oil and season with a little salt. Set aside in the fridge while baking the snapper, for the flavours to infuse.

Pour the rock salt into a roasting tin large enough to fit your fish. Tip in the egg whites and combine with the rock salt until you have the texture of wet sand. You can add up to 125 ml (4 fl oz/½ cup) water, if necessary.

Peel the rind from the lemon, avoiding the white pith, and add to the salt slurry along with the coriander seeds. Mix well with your hands, then form a thin layer across your roasting tin where your fish will sit, pushing the remaining salt to the edges. Lay your fish on top and drizzle a little olive oil over it.

Slice the peeled lemon half and stuff it into the cavity of the fish, along with the herbs. Pile the salt mixture onto the fish until it is completely covered in a layer of salt at least 1 cm (½ inch) thick.

Transfer to the oven and roast for 25–30 minutes, or until a knife inserted into the thickest part of the fish feels hot to the touch.

Remove from the oven and allow the fish to rest for 10 minutes.

Crack the salt crust with a knife and peel back the skin. Serve the fish with the salsa verde, and, if you like, some crusty bread and a simple green salad.

PROSCIUTTO-WRAPPED FISH WITH SICILIAN OLIVES & CHERRY TOMATOES

SERVES 4

400 g (14 oz) mixed cherry tomatoes

140 g (5 oz) Sicilian olives

1 tablespoon olive oil

60 g (2 oz) butter, softened

1 lemon, zested, then quartered

¾ teaspoon chilli flakes

8 slices prosciutto

4 × 150–170 g (5½–6 oz) skinless firm white fish fillets, such as rockling, cod or monkfish

Preheat the oven to 200°C/400°F (fan-forced). Lightly oil a roasting tin.

Toss the tomatoes and olives in the olive oil and season with salt and freshly ground black pepper. Set aside.

In a small bowl, mix the butter, lemon zest and chilli flakes until combined.

Lay one slice of prosciutto on a flat surface, and lay another slice on top, overlapping the first on the narrow end. Spoon a quarter of the butter mixture onto one of the slices, and spread evenly. Lay a piece of fish on top of the butter, then roll up the fish in the prosciutto. Place in the roasting tin, seam side down. Repeat with the remaining prosciutto, butter mixture and fish.

Arrange the tomatoes and olives around the fish, then roast for 8–10 minutes, or until the fish is cooked. The flesh will be opaque all the way through, and will flake easily when a piece is gently tested with a fork.

Serve immediately, with the tomatoes and olives.

TOMATO & CHORIZO BAKED FISH

SERVES 4

1 tablespoon olive oil
1 chorizo sausage, sliced
1 onion, diced
4 garlic cloves, crushed
1 teaspoon chilli flakes
1 tablespoon smoked paprika
2 bay leaves
1 teaspoon sugar
1 teaspoon salt
400 ml (14 fl oz) vegetable stock
1 × 400 g (14 oz) tin chopped tomatoes
4 × 150–170 g (5½–6 oz) skinless firm white fish
   fillets, such as rockling or blue grenadier
2 tablespoons lemon juice
2 tablespoons chopped parsley
crusty bread and lemon wedges, to serve

Preheat the oven to 170°C/340°F (fan-forced).

In a heavy-based ovenproof frying pan with a lid, heat the olive oil over medium heat. Add the chorizo, onion and garlic and fry for about 5 minutes, or until the chorizo releases its oil and the onion has softened.

Add the chilli flakes, paprika, bay leaves, sugar and salt, stirring well. Cook for 1–2 minutes, then stir in the stock and tomatoes. Bring to the boil.

Put the lid on, then transfer to the oven and cook for 30 minutes.

Remove from the oven and add the fish, gently submerging the fillets so the sauce has coated them all. Return to the oven and cook for a further 8–10 minutes, or until the fish is cooked through.

Remove from the oven, gently stir in the lemon juice, and scatter the parsley over the fish.

Serve with crusty bread to mop up the juices, and lemon wedges for squeezing over.

SALMON
EN CROUTE

SERVES 6

600–700 g (1 lb 5 oz–1 lb 9 oz) side of salmon,
   pin-boned, skin removed
1 tablespoon olive oil
1 French shallot, finely chopped
1 garlic clove, finely chopped
250 g (9 oz) English spinach, chopped
75 g (2¾ oz) watercress, chopped
small handful dill, finely chopped
small handful chives, finely chopped
1 dill pickle, finely diced
1 tablespoon crème fraîche
2 tablespoons dijon mustard
zest of 1 lemon
2 large sheets of puff pastry, or a 500 g
   (1 lb 2 oz) block cut in half, both halves
   rolled out to 5 mm (¼ inch) thick
1 free-range egg, beaten with 1 tablespoon milk
green salad, to serve

Preheat the oven to 170°C/340°F (fan-forced).

If you have a long piece of salmon, cut it in half crossways. If you have a fat, squat piece of salmon, make a deep incision along one side of the fillet, about halfway down, but not all the way through, to 'butterfly' it open, leaving a bit of a hinge.

Heat the olive oil in a frying pan over medium heat. Add the shallot and garlic and cook, stirring frequently, until lightly browned. Add the spinach and watercress and cook, stirring, until wilted. Remove from the heat and set aside in a sieve to drain.

Combine the herbs, dill pickle, crème fraîche, mustard and lemon zest in a bowl. Squeeze as much liquid as possible from the spinach mixture and add to the bowl. Season with salt and freshly ground black pepper and stir well to combine.

Depending on how you've prepared your fish, either fill the salmon cavity or place the spinach mixture on top of one salmon fillet. Place the other fillet on top or close the cavity.

Place the salmon on top of a pastry sheet. Brush the edges with the egg wash, then place the other pastry sheet on top and seal. You may need to trim the edges if you have too much pastry. Crimp the pastry edges together to seal, then brush all over with the egg wash. Cut shallow slashes across the top of the pastry parcel.

Transfer to the oven and bake for 30 minutes, or until the pastry is golden.

Remove from the oven and leave to rest for 10 minutes, then slice and serve with a green salad.

ROASTED SHELLFISH PLATTER

SERVES 4–6

500 g (1 lb 2 oz) clams (vongole)
2 cooked crabs
100 ml (3½ fl oz) olive oil
75 g (2¾ oz) butter
4 garlic cloves, crushed
large handful parsley, roughly chopped
1 raw lobster tail, sliced in half lengthways
12 large tiger prawns (shrimp), kept whole and
    unpeeled
1 kg (2 lb 3 oz) mussels, scrubbed well, beards
    removed
crusty white bread, to serve
2 lemons, cut into wedges

SAFFRON MAYONNAISE

pinch of saffron threads
1 large free-range egg yolk
½ teaspoon dijon mustard
up to 160 ml (5½ fl oz) neutral-flavoured oil,
    such as grapeseed or canola
juice of 1 lemon

Place the clams in a large bowl of cold water and soak for 1 hour .

To make the saffron mayonnaise, soak the saffron threads in 1 tablespoon hot water for about 10 minutes. Place the egg yolk, mustard and a large pinch of salt into the small bowl of a food processor. Process for about 1½ minutes, or until light and airy. With the motor running, slowly add the oil – drop by drop at first, then in a thin, steady stream, until you have a thick, glossy mayonnaise. Combine the lemon juice and saffron water and slowly pour the mixture in, processing until well combined. Set aside in the fridge.

Preheat the oven to 210°C/410°F (fan-forced).

Prepare the crabs by firmly lifting the base of the outer shell until it comes away completely. Rinse away the greyish material, snap off the 'apron' and mandibles at either end of the crab, and remove the gills in the middle. Slice each crab in half and use a meat mallet or rolling pin to smash the large front legs.

Pour 60 ml (2 fl oz/¼ cup) of the olive oil into a large roasting tin and place in the oven to heat up.

In a small saucepan, melt the butter and remaining oil over low heat and add the garlic and parsley. Set aside.

Place the lobster tail halves, flesh side down, in the hot roasting tin, along with the prawns. Roast in the oven for 3 minutes.

Meanwhile, drain the clams and rinse well. Tip the clams and mussels into another large roasting tin and add 60 ml (2 fl oz/ ¼ cup) water. Drizzle over half the melted garlic butter and place in the oven.

Remove the other roasting tin from the oven and flip the lobster and prawns over. Add the crab to the roasting tin and drizzle with the remaining melted garlic butter. Return to the oven and roast for a further 6–8 minutes, turning the prawns, mussels and clams every couple of minutes, until the mussels and clams have opened, and the lobster is cooked through.

Transfer the shellfish to a large serving platter, then drizzle with all the juices from both roasting tins. Serve immediately, with crusty white bread and the lemon wedges alongside.

LEMON-ROASTED PRAWNS WITH ROMESCO SAUCE

SERVES 4

60 ml (2 fl oz/¼ cup) olive oil
16 tiger prawns (shrimp), kept whole
    and unpeeled
2 garlic cloves, finely sliced
2 tablespoons chopped parsley
2 lemons, cut in half

ROMESCO SAUCE
1 dried ancho chilli
1 large tomato, cut in half
50 g (1¾ oz/ cup) blanched almonds
3 garlic cloves, peeled but left whole
1 slice crusty white bread, about 2 cm
    (¾ inch) thick
1 roasted red capsicum (bell pepper),
    from a jar (or see page 51)
about 80 ml (2½ fl oz/⅓ cup) olive oil
1 teaspoon smoked paprika
1½ tablespoons sherry vinegar
small handful parsley, chopped

Preheat the oven to 190°C/375°F (fan-forced). Line a tray with baking paper.

To make the romesco sauce, place the dried ancho chilli in a small bowl of hot water and set aside to soften for 20 minutes. Meanwhile, place the tomato halves on a baking tray, cut side up, along with the almonds, garlic cloves and bread. Roast in the oven for 15 minutes, turning the bread, almonds and garlic over now and then. Transfer the bread and almonds to a heatproof bowl and continue to roast the tomato and garlic for a further 15 minutes. Add them to the same bowl and set aside to cool. Increase the oven temperature to 200°C/400°F (fan-forced). Drain the ancho chilli, discard the seeds and finely chop the flesh. Transfer to the bowl of a small food processor, along with the roasted tomato, garlic and almonds. Tear the bread into smaller bits and add to the processor with the remaining romesco sauce ingredients. Blitz until you have a fine paste, adding a little more olive oil if necessary. Transfer to a bowl.

Pour the olive oil into a small roasting tin and place in the oven to heat up.

Combine the prawns, garlic and parsley in a bowl, then carefully transfer to the roasting tin, taking care as the oil will spit. Add the lemon halves, cut side down, and roast in the oven for 8 minutes, or until the prawns are firm and cooked through.

Transfer the prawns and their juices to a heatproof serving platter. Place the lemon halves on the side for squeezing over.

Serve immediately, with the romesco sauce for dipping the prawns into. Any leftover romesco will keep in an airtight container in the fridge for up to 5 days.

LIME, LEMONGRASS & CHILLI ROASTED SALMON

SERVES 4

large handful coriander (cilantro), stalks roughly chopped, leaves reserved for garnishing

5 garlic cloves, finely chopped

5 cm (2 inch) piece of fresh ginger, peeled and finely chopped

2 lemongrass stems, white part only, finely sliced

1 red chilli, finely chopped

1 tablespoon finely grated palm sugar (jaggery)

juice of 2 limes

2 tablespoons fish sauce

4 × 150 g (5½ oz) salmon fillets, pin-boned, skin removed

1 tablespoon sesame seeds, lightly toasted

Preheat the oven to 160°C/320°F (fan-forced).

Combine all the ingredients, except the salmon and sesame seeds, in a large bowl. Season well with salt and freshly ground black pepper. Add the salmon fillets and coat them thoroughly with the mixture.

Cover with plastic wrap and leave in the fridge for 20 minutes for the flavours to infuse.

Make four foil parcels and place a salmon fillet, skin side down, in each package. Spoon the marinating mixture over each one. Close up the foil parcels and seal tightly, then place on a baking tray.

Transfer to the oven and roast for 10 minutes, then remove from the oven and leave to rest for 2 minutes.

Transfer the fish to serving plates. Sprinkle with the toasted sesame seeds, garnish with the coriander leaves, drizzle over any remaining juices from the foil parcels and serve immediately.

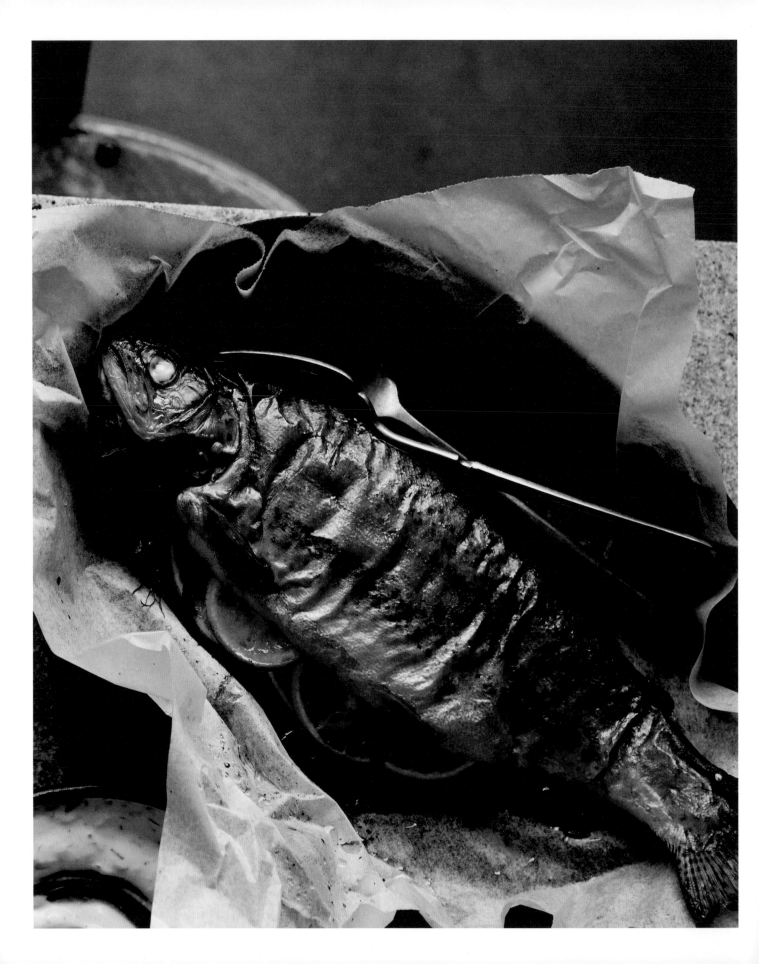

TRADITIONAL ROAST TROUT WITH HERBS & LEMON

SERVES 4

2 × 600 g (1 lb 5 oz) whole rainbow trout,
    scaled and cleaned
olive oil, for drizzling
small handful thyme
small handful dill
small handful oregano
1 lemon, finely sliced

HORSERADISH CREAM

60 g (2 oz) crème fraîche
60 g (2 oz/¼ cup) sour cream
2 teaspoons prepared horseradish (from a jar)
2 teaspoons dijon mustard
1 tablespoon finely chopped dill
juice of ½ lemon

Preheat the oven to 180°C/350°F (fan-forced). Line a large baking tray with baking paper.

To make the horseradish cream, combine all the ingredients in a small bowl and season well with salt and freshly ground black pepper. Taste, then adjust the flavours if necessary. Cover and set aside in the fridge while you prepare the trout.

Place each fish on the baking tray. Drizzle olive oil over each trout and inside the cavities. Stuff each fish with the herbs and lemon slices. Season well with salt and pepper.

Transfer to the oven and roast for 20 minutes.

Remove from the oven and allow the fish to rest for 2 minutes, then transfer to a serving platter.

Serve the fish in the middle of the table, with the horseradish cream on the side for everyone to help themselves.

ROAST CAJUN FISH

SERVES 4

4 × 150 g (5½ oz) thick firm white fish fillets,
  such as rockling or barramundi
50 g (1¾ oz) butter, melted
2 tablespoons olive oil

MANGO SALSA

2 garlic cloves, peeled but left whole
2 fresh jalapeño chillies
1 large mango, finely diced
¼ red onion, finely diced
½ red capsicum (bell pepper), finely diced
2 tablespoons chopped coriander (cilantro)
½ avocado, finely diced
juice of 1 lime

CAJUN SPICE MIX

1 tablespoon smoked paprika
2 teaspoons onion powder
2 teaspoons garlic powder
1 teaspoon cayenne pepper
2 teaspoons dried oregano
2 teaspoons dried basil
1½ teaspoons dried thyme
1 teaspoon ground white pepper
1 teaspoon freshly ground black pepper
2 teaspoons salt

Preheat the grill (broiler) to high.

To make the mango salsa, grill the garlic cloves and chillies for 12–15 minutes, or until well browned and blistered, turning occasionally. Set aside to cool. Combine the remaining ingredients in a bowl and season with salt and freshly ground black pepper. Remove the seeds from the chillies, then finely chop the flesh, along with the garlic. Stir through the salsa and check the seasoning. Set aside for 20 minutes for the flavours to infuse.

Meanwhile, preheat the oven to 180°C/350°F (fan-forced). Line a baking tray with foil.

To make the cajun spice mix, combine all the ingredients in a small bowl, mixing well.

Brush the fish with the melted butter, then coat well in the cajun spice mix. Heat the olive oil in a large frying pan over high heat and fry the fish for 1 minute on each side, or until blackened but not cooked through.

Transfer to the baking tray and bake for 6–8 minutes, depending on the thickness of the fish. The fish is cooked when the flesh is opaque all the way through, and flakes easily when gently tested with a fork.

Serve immediately, with the mango salsa.

WHOLE SNAPPER BAKED IN A SALT CRUST WITH SAFFRON MAYONNAISE

SERVES 4

1 kg (2 lb 3 oz) cooking salt
1.2 kg (2 lb 10 oz) whole snapper
1 lemon, sliced
1 lime, sliced
2 bay leaves
handful of dill sprigs
handful of flat-leaf (Italian) parsley leaves

SAFFRON MAYONNAISE

pinch of saffron threads
2 large free-range egg yolks
½ teaspoon dijon mustard
1 teaspoon cider vinegar
½ teaspoon sea salt flakes
pinch of freshly ground black pepper
250 ml (8½ fl oz/1 cup) light olive oil

Preheat the oven to 180°C/350°F (fan-forced).

Put the cooking salt in a large bowl. Add 250 ml (8½ fl oz/1 cup) water and mix together well.

On a large baking tray, form half the salt mixture into a fish shape, just larger than the snapper. Sit the fish on top. Place the lemon and lime slices into the cavity of the snapper, along with the bay leaves, dill and parsley. Press the remaining salt mixture over the fish, covering and sealing the fish completely.

Transfer to the oven and bake for 30 minutes.

Meanwhile, prepare the saffron mayonnaise. Soak the saffron threads in 1 tablespoon hot water for 15 minutes. In a bowl, combine the egg yolks, mustard, vinegar, salt and pepper. Whisk a few drops of the olive oil into the mixture. Continue adding small amounts of the oil, whisking well after each addition, until all the oil has been incorporated. Stir in the saffron threads and water, then taste and adjust the seasoning if required.

Remove the fish from the oven. Tap around the edge of the salt crust with the tip of a knife to loosen it, then lift the top off.

Transfer the snapper to a platter. Serve immediately, with the saffron mayonnaise.

COCONUT FISH CURRY

SERVES 4

4 garlic cloves, peeled
3 cm (1¼ inch) piece of fresh ginger, peeled
zest of 1 lime
3 lemongrass stems, white bases only, chopped
12 coriander (cilantro) roots, scrubbed clean
   (reserve the leaves for garnishing)
2 small red chillies, stems removed
1 teaspoon coconut oil
500 ml (17 fl oz/2 cups) coconut milk
½ teaspoon palm sugar (jaggery)
700 g (1 lb 9 oz) skinless firm white fish,
   cut into 5 cm (2 inch) chunks
2 teaspoons fish sauce
1 tablespoon lime juice
4 kaffir lime leaves, thinly sliced
steamed jasmine rice, to serve
3 spring onions (scallions), thinly sliced

Place the garlic, ginger, lime zest, lemongrass, coriander roots and chillies in a food processor and process to a coarse paste.

Heat the coconut oil in a wok over high heat and cook the spice paste for a minute or so, until fragrant. Add the coconut milk and palm sugar, reduce the heat to medium, and heat until simmering.

Add the fish and cook for 5 minutes, then stir in the fish sauce, lime juice and lime leaves. Remove from the heat.

Serve the curry in deep bowls on a bed of jasmine rice, garnished with the spring onion and reserved coriander leaves.

SALMON EN PAPILLOTE

SERVES 4

4 medium-sized boiling potatoes
2 garlic cloves, finely sliced
zest and juice of 2 lemons
2 tablespoons white wine
60 ml (2 fl oz/¼ cup) olive oil
4 × 150 g (5½ oz) salmon fillets, pin-boned,
  skin removed
1 large fennel bulb, sliced as thinly as possible
8 cornichons, cut in half lengthways
a few dill or fennel fronds, roughly chopped
green salad, to serve

Place the potatoes in a saucepan and cover with cold water. Season with salt and bring to the boil. Simmer for 8 minutes, or until just tender, then drain and set aside to cool slightly.

Meanwhile, preheat the oven to 180°C/350°F (fan-forced). Tear off four large sheets of baking paper and fold them into loose parcels.

Combine the garlic, lemon zest, lemon juice, wine and olive oil in a small screw-top jar. Season well with salt and freshly ground black pepper. Seal the jar and shake well.

Peel the potatoes, if you like, then thinly slice. Arrange the slices on the base of each parcel. Place a salmon fillet on top of each potato layer, then scatter with the fennel, cornichons and dill or fennel fronds. Give the dressing a good shake again and drizzle over the fish. Seal the parcels, making sure they are watertight.

Place the parcels on a baking tray, then into the oven. Bake for 12–15 minutes, or until the fish is just cooked through, and flakes easily when gently tested with a fork.

Serve immediately, with a green salad on the side.

TUNA PASTA BAKE WITH MUSHROOM, THYME & KALE

SERVES 4

400 g (14 oz) macaroni
2 tablespoons olive oil
1 garlic clove, finely chopped
250 g (9 oz) Swiss brown or portobello
    mushrooms, sliced
½ bunch kale, finely chopped
6 thyme sprigs, leaves picked
½ teaspoon sea salt flakes
2 × 185 g (6½ oz) tins of tuna in springwater,
    drained
200 g (7 oz) crème fraîche, light sour cream
    or pouring (single/light) cream (see note)
60 g (2 oz/½ cup) grated cheddar
3 tablespoons finely chopped flat-leaf
    (Italian) parsley
green salad, to serve

TOPPING

1 slice sourdough bread, broken roughly
    into crumbs
2 teaspoons olive oil
25 g (1 oz/¼ cup) grated parmesan

Preheat the oven to 140°C/275°F (fan-forced).

Bring a large saucepan of salted water to the boil over high heat. Add the macaroni and cook for 9 minutes, or until almost al dente; it will cook further in the oven. Drain the macaroni, reserving 60 ml (2 fl oz/¼ cup) of the cooking water.

Heat a large saucepan over medium heat. Add the olive oil, garlic and mushrooms and cook, stirring, for 4 minutes. Add the kale, thyme, salt and a good pinch of freshly ground black pepper. Cook, stirring, for a further 4 minutes, then remove from the heat.

Stir in the tuna, crème fraîche, cheddar and cooked macaroni, along with the reserved cooking water. Pour the mixture into a baking dish.

To make the topping, combine the sourdough crumbs and olive oil in a small bowl. Toss to coat the bread in the oil, then add the parmesan and mix together. Sprinkle the crumbs over the macaroni mixture and bake for 30 minutes, or until the crumbs are golden brown.

Scatter with the parsley and serve with a green salad.

✕ The advantage of using crème fraîche in recipes such as this is that it is far less likely to split during cooking than cream.

GREEK-STYLE SLOW-COOKED OCTOPUS

SERVES 4

1 x 1 kg (2 lb 3 oz) octopus
125 ml (4 fl oz/½ cup) dry white wine
80 ml (2½ fl oz/⅓ cup) olive oil
3 garlic cloves, crushed
1 red onion, finely chopped
300 g (10½ oz) pearl (baby) onions, peeled
1 tablespoon white wine vinegar
3 tomatoes, peeled and chopped
2 bay leaves
1 rosemary sprig
3 allspice berries
1 teaspoon peppercorns
2 teaspoons sea salt flakes
flat-leaf (Italian) parsley leaves, to garnish
crusty bread, to serve

Preheat the oven to 150°C/300°F (fan-forced).

To clean the octopus, use a sharp knife to separate the head from the tentacles, just below the eyes. Cut above the eyes, discard the eye segment, then remove and discard the contents of the head sac. Remove the beak from the centre of the body, where the tentacles join. Turn the head sac inside out and rinse it and the tentacles thoroughly.

Place the octopus in a large flameproof casserole dish. Add the wine, then cover and cook over high heat for 10 minutes. Remove the pan from the heat. Carefully lift the octopus onto a chopping board, retaining the cooking juices in the pan, and leave to cool.

To the cooking juices in the pan, add the olive oil, garlic, red onion and pearl onions. Cook over medium heat for 10 minutes, stirring occasionally.

Cut the octopus tentacles into 5 cm (2 inch) pieces, then add to the pan with the rest of the octopus. Add the vinegar, tomatoes, bay leaves, rosemary, allspice, peppercorns and salt.

Transfer to the oven and bake for 90 minutes, or until the octopus is very tender.

Garnish with parsley and serve with fresh crusty bread.

POULTRY

BAKED TARRAGON CHICKEN

SERVES 4

4 free-range chicken leg quarters
1½ tablespoons melted butter
3 tablespoons fresh tarragon leaves,
   or 1 tablespoon dried tarragon
2 lemons, quartered
2 large potatoes, peeled and quartered
green salad, to serve

Preheat the oven to 140°C/275°F (fan-forced).

Place the chicken pieces in a large baking dish and season with sea salt flakes and freshly ground black pepper. Brush with the melted butter, then sprinkle with the tarragon. Tuck the lemon quarters in and around the chicken.

Cover the baking dish tightly with foil, transfer to the oven and bake for 1½ hours.

Remove the foil and add the potatoes to the dish. Brush the chicken and potatoes with the cooking juices from the bottom of the dish.

Return to the oven, leaving the foil off, and bake for a further 1 hour.

Increase the oven temperature to 180°C/350°F (fan-forced). Bake for a final 20 minutes, or until the potatoes are cooked through and the chicken skin is golden.

Serve the chicken and potatoes with a green salad.

FRENCH-STYLE CHICKEN CASSEROLE

SERVES 4

4 free-range chicken thigh cutlets, skin on
4 free-range chicken drumsticks
25 g (1 oz) butter
2 tablespoons olive oil
4 French shallots, chopped
2 garlic cloves, finely chopped
1 carrot, cut in half lengthways, then thickly
   sliced
200 g (7 oz) portobello or Swiss brown
   mushrooms, quartered
2 bay leaves
3 thyme sprigs
250 ml (8½ fl oz/1 cup) riesling or dry white wine
375 ml (12½ fl oz/1½ cups) chicken stock
200 g (7 oz) potatoes, peeled and cut into
   small cubes
1 teaspoon tarragon leaves
80 g (2¾ oz/½ cup) freshly podded peas
chopped flat-leaf (Italian) parsley, to garnish
crusty bread, to serve

Preheat the oven to 130°C/265°F (fan-forced).

Season the chicken with sea salt flakes and freshly ground black pepper. Heat the butter and half the olive oil in a large heavy-based casserole dish. Working in batches if necessary, brown the chicken on both sides over high heat, then remove to a plate.

Add the remaining oil to the dish, then cook the shallot, garlic, carrot and mushrooms over medium heat for 5 minutes. Add the bay leaves, thyme sprigs and wine and simmer for 2 minutes.

Stir in the stock and bring to the boil. Return the chicken pieces to the dish, put the lid on, then place in the oven. Bake for 1½ hours.

Remove the dish from the oven. Add the potato and tarragon, then replace the lid and cook on the stove over low heat for 5–7 minutes, or until the potato is tender. Add the peas and simmer for 2–3 minutes, or until the peas are tender, but still bright green.

Remove and discard the bay leaves. Pick the leaves from the thyme sprigs and add them to the casserole. Garnish with parsley and serve with crusty bread.

PANANG CHICKEN CURRY

SERVES 4

1 tablespoon peanut oil
500 g (1 lb 2 oz) boneless, skinless chicken
    thighs, sliced very thinly
1 carrot, thinly sliced on the diagonal
1 small red capsicum (bell pepper),
    quartered and sliced
250 ml (8½ fl oz/1 cup) coconut milk
2 tomatoes, cut into wedges
juice of ½ lime
3 Thai basil sprigs, leaves picked
steamed jasmine rice, to serve

SPICE PASTE

40 g (1½ oz/¼ cup) raw peanuts
8 dried red chillies, seeds removed
1½ teaspoons coriander seeds
½ teaspoon cumin seeds
1 cardamom pod
1 teaspoon sea salt flakes
2 teaspoons chopped peeled galangal root
2 lemongrass stems, lower one-third only,
    chopped
3 kaffir lime leaves, chopped
1 tablespoon chopped coriander (cilantro) root
    (washed well before chopping)
1 red Asian shallot, finely chopped
3 garlic cloves, crushed
1 teaspoon fermented shrimp paste; if
    unavailable, use 1 tablespoon fish sauce

Start by making the spice paste. Place the peanuts and chillies in a heatproof bowl and cover with boiling water. Soak for 10 minutes, then drain and set aside.

Heat a small dry frying pan over medium heat and toast the coriander seeds, cumin seeds, cardamom pod and salt for a minute or two until fragrant, stirring so the spices don't burn.

Place the toasted spices into a mortar and grind them using a pestle. Add the drained peanuts and chillies, along with the galangal, lemongrass, lime leaves and coriander root. Pound until a smooth paste forms, then add the shallot, garlic and shrimp paste and pound again until smooth.

Heat a wok over medium heat and add the peanut oil and spice paste. Fry for a minute or so, stirring often, until fragrant. Add the chicken and stir-fry for 2 minutes, then add the carrot and capsicum and stir-fry for a further minute.

Stir in the coconut milk and tomato wedges and leave to simmer for 5 minutes.

Remove from the heat, then stir in the lime juice and basil leaves. Serve over jasmine rice.

SLOW-COOKED CHICKEN ENCHILADAS

Heat the stock and garlic in a saucepan over medium heat until almost boiling. Add the chicken and cover the pan, then reduce the heat to low and simmer for 1 hour. Transfer the chicken to a bowl and set aside.

Add the tomatillos and jalapeño chillies to the stock. Bring back to a simmer and cook for 15 minutes, or until the chillies are tender. Allow to cool a little, then strain the mixture through a sieve, into a bowl, retaining the stock.

Meanwhile, preheat the oven to 160°C/320°F (fan-forced).

Place the tomatillos, jalapeño chillies and garlic cloves in a blender. Add the onion and salt and process until a rough sauce forms. Add 170 ml (5½ fl oz/2⁄3 cup) of the reserved stock and process until well blended.

Shred the chicken finely. Place in a bowl and add 250 ml (8½ fl oz/1 cup) of the tomatillo sauce, stirring to coat the chicken in the sauce.

Lay the tortillas on a clean board. Place the chicken mixture along the centre of each tortilla, dividing it evenly. Roll the tortilla sides up and over to enclose the filling, then lay the enchiladas in a baking dish. Pour the remaining tomatillo sauce over the top. Spoon the crema down the centre, then sprinkle with the cheese. Bake for 20–25 minutes, or until completely heated through.

Meanwhile, combine the salsa ingredients together in a small bowl. Serve the enchiladas straight from the oven, with the salsa.

SERVES 4–6

500 ml (17 fl oz/2 cups) chicken stock
2 garlic cloves, smashed
500 g (1 lb 2 oz) boneless, skinless chicken thighs
800 g (1 lb 12 oz) tinned tomatillos, drained
2 jalapeño chillies, stems removed
1 small white onion, chopped
1 teaspoon sea salt flakes
8 large corn tortillas
185 ml (6½ fl oz/¾ cup) Mexican crema (see note) or light sour cream
25 g (1 oz/¼ cup) grated Manchego or parmesan

FRESH SALSA

1 small white onion, finely chopped
1 jalapeño chilli, seeds removed, finely chopped
25 g (1 oz/½ cup) finely chopped coriander (cilantro) leaves

✕ Mexican crema is a cultured cream used widely in that cuisine. It can be made in batches and stored in the fridge for 2 weeks. To make crema for this recipe, blend 60 ml (2 fl oz/¼ cup) buttermilk, yoghurt or sour cream with 125 ml (4 fl oz/½ cup) thick (double/heavy) cream and a pinch of sea salt. Cover and store at room temperature for 6–8 hours, or overnight. The crema can then be refrigerated until needed. Serve at room temperature.

CREAMY CALVADOS CHICKEN

SERVES 4

1 tablespoon olive oil

2 teaspoons butter

2 French shallots, finely chopped

1 streaky bacon slice, finely chopped

4 free-range chicken drumsticks

4 free-range chicken thigh cutlets, bone in

2 tablespoons Calvados (see note)

125 ml (4 fl oz/½ cup) apple cider

3 lemon thyme sprigs

2 pink eating apples, cored and cut into
6 wedges each

1 teaspoon sea salt flakes

¼ teaspoon freshly ground black pepper

80 g (2¾ oz/⅓ cup) crème fraîche, light sour
cream or pouring (single/light) cream

3 tablespoons finely chopped flat-leaf
(Italian) parsley

steamed new potatoes, to serve

green salad, to serve

Heat the olive oil and butter in a large heavy-based saucepan over medium heat. Add the shallot and bacon and cook for 5 minutes, or until the shallot has softened and the bacon is beginning to crisp.

Add the chicken and cook for 2–3 minutes on each side. Add the Calvados and stir to deglaze the pan.

Stir in the cider, lemon thyme sprigs, apple wedges, salt and pepper. Cover and cook over low heat for 45 minutes, or until the chicken is cooked through and tender. Check the pan occasionally, adding a tablespoon or two of water if it becomes dry.

Gently stir in the crème fraîche. Allow to simmer for a further minute, then remove from the heat.

Sprinkle with the parsley and serve with steamed potatoes and a fresh green salad.

✗ Calvados is an apple brandy from the Normandy region in northern France. If you don't have any, simply leave it out, or use Armagnac or brandy instead.

CHICKEN CACCIATORE

SERVES 4

4 free-range chicken leg quarters, or 4 chicken
    drumsticks and 4 thigh cutlets, skin on
100 g (3½ oz) pancetta, chopped
2 tablespoons olive oil
1 large onion, finely chopped
2 large garlic cloves, finely chopped
200 g (7 oz) Swiss brown or button mushrooms,
    quartered
1 red capsicum (bell pepper), thinly sliced
2 bay leaves
2 thyme sprigs
185 ml (6½ fl oz/¾ cup) white or red wine
400 g (14 oz) tinned cherry tomatoes or
    crushed tomatoes
250 ml (8½ fl oz/1 cup) chicken stock
12 pitted kalamata olives
½ teaspoon sugar
chopped flat-leaf (Italian) parsley or basil,
    to serve
crusty bread, crunchy roasted potatoes or
    mashed potato, to serve

Heat a large heavy-based or cast-iron saucepan over high heat. Brown the chicken on both sides for 3–4 minutes (you won't need any oil in the pan at this stage, as there is plenty of fat in the skin). Remove the chicken to a plate.

Add the pancetta to the pan and cook, stirring, over high heat for 2 minutes.

Reduce the heat to medium. Add the olive oil, onion, garlic and mushrooms and sauté for 5 minutes, or until the onion has softened and the mushrooms have coloured. Add the capsicum and cook for 2 minutes, until softened. Now add the bay leaves and thyme sprigs, and return the chicken to the pan.

Pour in the wine, then allow to bubble for 3–4 minutes to reduce slightly. Stir in the tomatoes and stock, then cover and simmer over low heat for 1 hour.

Remove the lid and simmer for a further 5 minutes, or until the sauce has reduced slightly. Stir in the olives and sugar, then season to taste with sea salt flakes and freshly ground black pepper.

Garnish with parsley and serve with your choice of accompaniment.

MOROCCAN-SPICED ROAST CHICKEN WITH PRESERVED LEMON

SERVES 4

1 large red capsicum (bell pepper)
600 g (1 lb 5 oz) new potatoes, scrubbed
4 French shallots, peeled
1 tablespoon olive oil
1 x 1.5–1.7 kg (3 lb 5 oz–3 lb 12 oz) whole
   free-range chicken
250 g (9 oz) green beans

SPICED LEMON BUTTER

60 g (2 oz) butter, softened
½ teaspoon freshly ground black pepper
½ teaspoon salt
¼ teaspoon sumac
½ teaspoon ground coriander
¼ teaspoon ground cinnamon
½ teaspoon ground cumin
½ teaspoon smoked paprika
½ teaspoon chilli flakes
½ preserved lemon, rinsed, flesh discarded,
   rind finely diced

Preheat the oven to 180°C/350°F (fan-forced).

Cut the capsicum into eight even-sized pieces. Remove and discard the seeds and membrane then place in a bowl with the whole potatoes and shallots. Add the olive oil and toss until the vegetables are coated. Season with salt and freshly ground black pepper and set aside.

To make the spiced lemon butter, mix together all the ingredients in a small bowl until well combined.

Use a spoon or your fingers to very gently separate the chicken skin from the breast, and the top of the thighs. Push three-quarters of the spiced butter under the skin, smoothing out to ensure it is evenly distributed. Rub the remaining butter on the outside of the skin.

Place the chicken in a roasting tin, transfer to the oven and roast for 20 minutes.

Add the potatoes and shallots to the roasting tin and roast for a further 40 minutes. Add the capsicum and roast for a final 20 minutes; the chicken needs to roast for 1 hour 20 minutes in total.

Leaving the vegetables in the roasting tin, transfer the chicken to a plate, cover loosely with foil and leave to rest for 15 minutes.

Meanwhile, add the green beans to the roasting tin and roast for 15 minutes.

Serve the chicken drizzled with any juices from the roasting tin, with the roasted vegetables alongside.

BUTTER
CHICKEN

SERVES 4

125 g (4½ oz/½ cup) plain yoghurt
1 tablespoon lemon juice
2 teaspoons garam masala
500 g (1 lb 2 oz) boneless, skinless chicken
   thighs, cut into 3 cm (1¼ inch) chunks
1 tablespoon vegetable oil
2 garlic cloves, crushed
3 cm (1¼ inch) piece of fresh ginger,
   peeled and grated
2 small dried chillies
1 cinnamon stick
1 teaspoon sea salt flakes
1 teaspoon ground coriander
1 teaspoon ground cumin
¼ teaspoon ground turmeric
185 ml (6½ fl oz/¾ cup) tomato passata
1 teaspoon sugar
1½ tablespoons almond meal
185 ml (6½ fl oz/¾ cup) pouring (single/light)
   cream
steamed basmati rice, to serve
coriander (cilantro) leaves, to garnish

Combine the yoghurt, lemon juice and garam masala in a bowl. Add the chicken and mix until well coated. Cover and refrigerate for 6 hours or overnight.

Heat the vegetable oil in a large saucepan over medium heat. Add the garlic, ginger, chillies, cinnamon stick, salt, coriander, cumin and turmeric. Cook, stirring, for 1 minute, or until fragrant. Add the chicken and cook for 3–4 minutes, stirring well to coat it in the spices.

Stir in the passata, sugar and almond meal, then cover and simmer over low heat for 20 minutes.

Stir in the cream, then remove from the heat.

Serve with basmati rice, garnished with coriander.

MUSHROOM-STUFFED CHICKEN BREASTS WITH GARLIC CREAM SAUCE

Heat 1 tablespoon of the olive oil in a frying pan over medium heat and fry the mushrooms for 3–4 minutes, or until cooked. Transfer to a bowl, along with the cheese and breadcrumbs. Season with salt and freshly ground black pepper, mix together and set aside to cool.

Preheat the oven to 180°C/350°F (fan-forced).

Lay a chicken breast flat on a chopping board, with the smooth round side facing downwards. Being careful not to slice all the way through, use a sharp knife to make a small cut along the join where the tenderloin meets the breast, to flatten slightly. Now push the blade from the side near the join, into the thickest part of the breast, and draw downwards, to create a pocket within the breast. Gently push one-quarter of the mushroom stuffing into the pocket, then pull the tenderloin over the join, creating a 'lid' for the opening. Wrap a slice of bacon around the stuffed breast, securing with a toothpick if needed. Repeat with the remaining chicken breasts, stuffing and bacon.

Heat the remaining oil in a large frying pan, then brown the bacon-wrapped chicken breasts for about 2 minutes on each side.

Transfer to a roasting tin and roast for 30–40 minutes, or until the internal temperature of the chicken reaches 75°C (167°F) on a meat thermometer.

Meanwhile, make the garlic cream sauce. Heat the olive oil in a frying pan over medium heat and fry the garlic for 1 minute. Increase the heat to high, add the wine and bring to the boil. Reduce the heat to medium and simmer until the liquid has reduced by half. Stir in the cream and continue to simmer until the liquid has again reduced by half, and the sauce has thickened.

Allow the chicken to rest for 5 minutes, then slice each breast into rounds. Serve with the sauce.

SERVES 4

2 tablespoons olive oil
220 g (8 oz) mushrooms, diced
100 g (3½ oz) cheddar, grated
55 g (2 oz/⅔ cup) fresh breadcrumbs
4 free-range chicken breast fillets
4 slices middle bacon

GARLIC CREAM SAUCE

1 tablespoon olive oil
3 garlic cloves, crushed
250 ml (8½ fl oz/1 cup) white wine
250 ml (8½ fl oz/1 cup) pouring cream

CHUNKY CHICKEN POT PIES

MAKES 4

1 egg, beaten
salad or vegetables, to serve

ROUGH PUFF PASTRY

225 g (8 oz) cold butter, cut into small cubes
225 g (8 oz/1½ cups) plain (all-purpose) flour,
  plus extra for dusting
½ teaspoon sea salt flakes
80 ml (2½ fl oz/⅓ cup) cold water, mixed with
  a squeeze of lemon

FILLING

1 tablespoon olive oil
700 g (1 lb 9 oz) skinless chicken thigh fillets,
  trimmed and cut into 2.5–3 cm (1–1¼ inch)
  chunks
2 leeks, white part only, cut in half lengthways,
  then chopped
1 medium–large carrot, chopped
1 celery stalk, chopped
1 large garlic clove, finely chopped
3 lemon thyme or thyme sprigs
1 bay leaf
125 ml (4 fl oz/½ cup) dry white wine
250 ml (8½ fl oz/1 cup) chicken stock
185 ml (6½ fl oz/¾ cup) thickened (whipping)
  cream
1 teaspoon dijon mustard
1 tablespoon chopped tarragon or sage
50 g (1¾ oz) spinach, thickly shredded

To make the pastry, roughly rub the butter cubes into the flour and salt, without overworking – there should still be small lumps of butter. Make a well in the centre. Gradually add the cold water, mixing it in with your hands to form a dough. Shape the dough into a disc, wrap in plastic wrap and rest in the fridge for 30 minutes.

On a floured surface, roll the dough out into a rectangle 1.5 cm (½ inch) thick. Fold one of the short ends of the dough two-thirds of the way into the centre. Fold the remaining pastry third back over to the opposite end, to form a book shape. Wrap and chill again for 25 minutes. Repeat this folding process twice more. After the final folding, ensure the pastry has rested in the fridge for at least 30 minutes before using.

Meanwhile make the filling. Heat the oil in a saucepan and brown the chicken over high heat for 8–10 minutes. Add the leek, carrot, celery and garlic and cook over medium heat for 5 minutes, or until the vegetables soften. Add the thyme and bay leaf and season with salt and pepper. Stir in the wine and cook for 2–3 minutes, or until reduced by half, then add the stock. Cover and leave to cook over low heat for 45 minutes.

Remove the lid from the pan. Stir in the cream and simmer gently for a further 25 minutes. Remove and discard the thyme and bay leaf. Stir in the mustard and tarragon, then stir the spinach through until wilted. Remove from the heat and leave to cool.

Preheat the oven to 180°C/350°F (fan-forced).

Roll the pastry out to 1 cm (½ inch) thick. Divide the chicken mixture among four 250 ml (8½ fl oz/1 cup) ramekins. Brush around the rim with beaten egg, so the pastry will adhere. Place a ramekin on the pastry and cut out a circle a bit larger than the ramekin. Place the pastry over the filling, pressing the dough down around the outside of the ramekin. Repeat with the remaining pastry, until all the pies are topped. Using a knife, make a small slit in the centre of each pie lid, to allow steam to escape.

Bake for 30 minutes, or until the pastry is golden and puffed. Serve hot, with salad or vegetables.

CHICKEN WITH 40 CLOVES OF GARLIC & LEMON GARLIC GRAVY

SERVES 4

8 free-range chicken thighs, skin on
   and bone in
1 tablespoon olive oil
20 g (¾ oz) butter
190 ml (6½ fl oz/¾ cup) white wine
250 ml (8½ fl oz/1 cup) chicken stock
40 garlic cloves, unpeeled
8 thyme sprigs
1 bay leaf
1 lemon, cut in half
1 tablespoon plain (all-purpose) flour
crusty bread, to serve

Preheat the oven to 160°C/320°F (fan-forced).

Pat the chicken thighs dry with paper towel. Place a flameproof casserole dish, large enough to fit all the chicken in a single layer, over medium–high heat; you'll need one with a tight-fitting lid. Add the olive oil and butter then add half the chicken, skin side down, and brown well for about 5 minutes. Turn the chicken and brown the other side for about 3–4 minutes. Remove to a plate and brown the remaining chicken pieces in the same way, then add them to the plate.

Drain the excess fat from the dish. Reduce the heat, add the wine and leave to simmer for 1–2 minutes.

Stir in the stock, scatter in a handful of the garlic cloves, then return all the chicken to the dish, fitting it in snugly in a single layer. Add the thyme sprigs, bay leaf and lemon halves, then tuck the remaining garlic cloves in around the chicken.

Remove the casserole dish from the heat. Cover with a double layer of foil, tightly sealing the edges, then place the lid on. Transfer to the oven and roast for 1¼ hours.

Remove the dish from the oven. Transfer the chicken and garlic to a plate, leaving about 10 cloves of garlic and all the juices in the dish. Loosely cover the chicken with foil to keep warm.

Using a spoon, press down on the garlic cloves in the casserole dish to release them from their skins. Discard the skins, and mash the garlic into the juices.

Place the dish back over medium–high heat. Mix 2–3 tablespoons of the juices with the flour until smooth, then add to the dish and stir well, cooking for a few minutes until the gravy has thickened. Remove from the heat and return the chicken and garlic cloves to the dish. Serve with crusty bread, to mop up all the juices, and to spread the garlic over.

SPICY ROASTED CHICKEN WITH BLUE CHEESE SAUCE

SERVES 4

100 g (3½ oz/⅔ cup) plain (all-purpose) flour

2 teaspoons garlic powder

2 teaspoons salt

1 teaspoon freshly ground black pepper

1 teaspoon smoked paprika

1.5 kg (3 lb 5 oz) chicken pieces, a mix of wingettes and drumettes

100 ml (3½ fl oz) hot sauce, such as Tabasco

75 g (2¾ oz) butter, melted

BLUE CHEESE SAUCE

125 g (4½ oz/½ cup) sour cream

130 g (4½ oz) whole-egg mayonnaise

1 large garlic clove, crushed

100 g (3½ oz) stilton

100 g (3½ oz) mild blue cheese

Preheat the oven to 200°C/400°F (fan-forced).

Place the flour, garlic powder, salt, pepper and paprika in a large zip-lock bag. Working in batches, toss the chicken pieces in the bag, ensuring each is evenly coated. Remove from the bag, shaking off the excess, and place on a roasting rack over a baking tray.

Transfer to the oven and roast for 35 minutes.

When the chicken is nearly ready, place all the ingredients for the blue cheese sauce in the small bowl of a food processor and process into a smooth sauce. Transfer to a small bowl and set aside until ready to serve.

When the chicken is done, remove from the oven. In a large bowl, mix the hot sauce with the melted butter, then add the chicken pieces and toss to coat.

Serve immediately, with the blue cheese sauce.

CHICKEN IN COCONUT MILK

SERVES 4

60 ml (2 fl oz/¼ cup) olive oil
1 x 1.5–1.7 kg (3 lb 5 oz–3 lb 12 oz) free-range
   whole chicken, cut into 8 pieces
grated zest and juice of ½ lime
400 ml (14 fl oz) coconut milk
250 ml (8½ fl oz/1 cup) chicken stock
2 teaspoons grated palm sugar (jaggery)
small piece of fresh ginger, peeled and
   thickly sliced
1 lemongrass stem, trimmed and bashed
4 garlic cloves, sliced
½ teaspoon chilli flakes
coriander (cilantro), to serve

Preheat the oven to 180°C/350°F (fan-forced).

Heat a large flameproof casserole dish over medium–high heat. Add the olive oil and brown the chicken on all sides, for about 5–6 minutes.

Turn off the heat, then drain off and discard the oil from the dish.

Sprinkle the lime zest over the chicken, then gently squeeze the half-lime over. Mix together the coconut milk, stock, sugar, ginger, lemongrass, garlic and chilli flakes and pour over the chicken.

Put the lid on, transfer to the oven and roast for 15 minutes. Baste the chicken with the sauce, put the lid back on and bake for a further 15 minutes.

Remove the lid and cook for a further 15 minutes, or until the skin is nicely browned and the internal temperature of the chicken reaches 75°C (167°F) on a meat thermometer.

Transfer the chicken to a serving dish. Pour the sauce over the chicken, garnish with coriander and serve.

ROAST CHICKEN WITH WALNUT & SAGE STUFFING & PARSNIP GRAVY

SERVES 4

1 carrot
1 large onion
2 parsnips
2 celery stalks
4 garlic cloves, unpeeled
1 x 1.5–1.7 kg (3 lb 5 oz–3 lb 12 oz)
    free-range chicken
15 g (¾ oz) butter
about 170 ml (5½ fl oz/⅔ cup) white wine
250 ml (8½ fl oz/1 cup) chicken stock,
    plus a little extra
1 tablespoon plain (all-purpose) flour

HERB BUTTER

60 g (2 oz) butter, softened
1 teaspoon chopped sage
1 teaspoon chopped parsley

Preheat the oven to 180°C/350°F (fan-forced). Line a baking tray with baking paper.

Peel the carrot, onion and parsnips. Roughly chop them, along with the celery, and place in a roasting tin with the unpeeled garlic cloves.

To make the herb butter, place the butter in a small bowl. Add the sage and parsley, season with salt and freshly ground black pepper and mix well with a fork.

Use a spoon or your fingers to very gently separate the chicken skin from the breast, and the top of the thighs. Push three-quarters of the herb butter under the skin, smoothing out to ensure it is evenly distributed. Rub the remaining herb butter on the outside of the skin, and season with salt and pepper.

Place the chicken in the roasting tin, on top of the vegetables. Transfer to the oven and roast for 40 minutes.

Meanwhile, make the stuffing. Melt the butter in a frying pan over medium heat, then fry the bacon, onion and sage for about 5 minutes, or until the onion is softened and the bacon is cooked. Transfer to a bowl, add the breadcrumbs, walnuts and parsley, season well with salt and freshly ground black pepper, and stir to combine. Add the eggs and mix well. Using your hands, shape the mixture into 12 evenly sized balls, and place on a baking tray lined with baking paper until ready to cook.

Once the chicken has roasted for 40 minutes, remove from the oven and add the wine and stock to the roasting tin. Roast for a further 40 minutes, or until the chicken reaches an internal temperature of 75°C (167°F) when tested with a meat thermometer, adding the tray of stuffing balls to the oven with 5 minutes to go.

Remove the roasting tin from the oven. Transfer the chicken to a plate, cover loosely with foil and leave to rest for 15 minutes while the stuffing finishes cooking, and you make the gravy.

Strain the juices from the roasting tin, into a measuring jug.

Take the parsnips and garlic from the roasting tin. Peel the garlic. Purée the parsnips and garlic with the strained roasting tin juices, using a hand-held stick blender or a blender.

Strain the liquid back into the measuring jug, adding a little extra stock if needed to top up the liquid level to 375 ml (12½ fl oz/ 1½ cups).

Discard any solids remaining in the roasting tin. Melt the butter in the roasting tin over low heat, then add the flour and stir until it becomes a smooth paste. Cook for 2–3 minutes, then add the stock gradually, stirring until you have a thickened sauce, ensuring any bits stuck to the bottom of the tin are scraped off and mixed into the gravy. Stir in any juices that have collected from the chicken during resting.

When ready to serve, carve the chicken and serve with the gravy.

WALNUT & SAGE STUFFING

40 g (1½ oz) butter
200 g (7 oz) bacon, diced
1 large onion, diced
14 sage leaves, shredded
240 g (8½ oz/3 cups) fresh breadcrumbs
100 g (3½ oz/1 cup) walnuts, chopped
3 teaspoons chopped parsley
2 free-range eggs, beaten

ROAST CHICKEN WITH
WALNUT & SAGE STUFFING
& PARSNIP GRAVY
×

SPICED POUSSIN WITH HERBED YOGHURT

SERVES 4

4 poussin, weighing about 500 g
(1 lb 2 oz) each
2 teaspoons ground cumin
1 tablespoon ground turmeric
½ teaspoon ground coriander
½ teaspoon garam masala
½ teaspoon salt
½ teaspoon freshly ground black pepper
2 tablespoons olive oil
125 g (4½ oz/½ cup) Greek-style yoghurt
2 garlic cloves, crushed
juice of 1 lemon

HERBED YOGHURT

250 g (9 oz/1 cup) Greek-style yoghurt
1 tablespoon chopped mint
1 tablespoon chopped coriander
(cilantro) leaves
1 tablespoon chopped parsley
1 garlic clove, crushed

Using kitchen string, truss the legs of each poussin together.

In a small bowl, mix together the spices, olive oil, yoghurt, garlic and lemon juice until well combined. Massage the mixture over each poussin, then transfer to the fridge to marinate for 2 hours.

Preheat the oven to 160°C/320°F (fan-forced).

Place the poussin in a roasting tin and roast for 45–55 minutes, or until the juices run clear when tested with a skewer, inserted into the thickest part of the thigh.

Remove from the oven, cover lightly with foil and leave to rest for 10 minutes.

Meanwhile, to make the herbed yoghurt, combine all ingredients in a small bowl, mixing well.

Serve the poussin with the herbed yoghurt.

ROAST QUAIL WITH BAKED FIGS, FETA & PISTACHIOS

SERVES 4–6

6 fresh figs, cut in half
olive oil, for drizzling and brushing
6 quail, spatchcocked/butterflied
2 tablespoons pomegranate molasses,
   plus extra to serve
100 g (3½ oz/⅔ cup) crumbled feta
2 tablespoons pistachio nuts, roughly
   chopped or slivered
fresh pomegranate seeds, to serve

Preheat the oven to 160°C/320°F (fan-forced). Line a large roasting tin with baking paper.

Heat a large chargrill pan over high heat. Drizzle the figs with a little olive oil and place on the hot pan, cut side down. Cook for 1–2 minutes, or until marked, then set aside.

Season the quail with salt and freshly ground black pepper and brush with olive oil. Working in batches if necessary, chargrill the quail, skin side down, for 3–4 minutes, or until well browned, then turn and cook the other side for a further 1 minute.

Transfer to the roasting tin, skin side up, along with the figs. Drizzle all over with the pomegranate molasses and roast for 5–8 minutes, or until the quail is cooked through.

Transfer the quail to a warm plate and cover loosely with foil to rest for a few minutes.

Serve the quail with the figs, scattered with the feta, pistachios and pomegranate seeds. Drizzle with any pan juices and a little extra pomegranate molasses.

X To spatchcock/butterfly the quail, cut along both sides of the spine with kitchen scissors and discard the backbone (or save for making stock). Open the quail out, skin side up, and press gently with the heel of your hand to flatten. Tuck the wing tips underneath.

ROAST GOOSE WITH CHESTNUT & APPLE STUFFING

SERVES 6

1 × 3.5–4 kg (7 lb 12 oz–8 lb 13 oz) whole goose
1 tablespoon olive oil
1 lemon, cut in half
1 rosemary sprig
2 sage sprigs
Brussels sprouts with cannellini beans
    and crumbled pancetta (page 265),
    to serve (optional)

CHESTNUT & APPLE STUFFING LOAF

20 g (¾ oz) butter
1 tablespoon olive oil
1 onion, finely chopped
2 garlic cloves, crushed
200 g (7 oz) pork sausages, removed from
    their casings
140 g (5 oz/2 cups) fresh sourdough
    breadcrumbs
70 g (2½ oz/½ cup) frozen prepared chestnuts,
    thawed and roughly chopped
1 apple, grated
2 tablespoons shredded sage leaves
large handful parsley, chopped
finely grated zest of 1 orange
1 free-range egg, beaten

Preheat the oven to 200°C/400°F (fan-forced).

Fold the wings under the goose. Open the vent at the leg end and drain any liquid from the cavity. Remove any excess fat and cut off the neck. Dry the skin with paper towel and season the goose, inside and out, with salt and pepper. Rub the seasoning into the skin, then rub the goose all over with the olive oil. Place the lemon halves, rosemary and sage sprigs in the cavity. Place the goose on a rack in a roasting tin and roast for 20 minutes.

Meanwhile, start making the stuffing. Heat the butter and oil in a large frying pan over medium heat. Add the onion and garlic and cook for 6–8 minutes, or until the onion is softened. Transfer to a large bowl and set aside to cool.

When the goose has roasted for 20 minutes, reduce the oven temperature to 160°C/320°F (fan-forced). Roast for a further 2 hours 20 minutes, or until the legs pull away easily, or a meat thermometer registers 75°C (167°F) when you test the meat in several places.

About 15 minutes before the goose is done, add the remaining stuffing ingredients to the sautéed onion mixture. Mix well and season to taste. Butter a small loaf (bar) tin and either spoon the stuffing into it, or form it into a log shape on a piece of baking paper and place it in the tin. Drizzle with a little goose fat from the main roasting tin.

The stuffing will take about 40 minutes to cook through, so add it to the oven about 10 minutes before the goose is done. At this time you could also add any root vegetables you'd like to roast and serve with the goose.

When the goose has finished cooking, transfer it to a warm plate, cover loosely with foil and leave to rest for 30 minutes. Meanwhile, leave the stuffing in the oven for a further 30 minutes, or until lightly browned and just firm to touch.

Carve the goose and serve with slices of stuffing, and, if you like, a side of brussels sprouts.

ROLLED TURKEY BREAST WITH LEMON & HERB STUFFING

SERVES 10–12

1 × 2 kg (4 lb 6 oz) turkey breast fillet
(unfilled turkey breast roll)
1 tablespoon olive oil
sage leaves, to garnish
Spicy cranberry sauce (see page 141),
to serve (optional)

LEMON & HERB STUFFING

20 g (¾ oz) butter
1 tablespoon olive oil
1 onion, finely chopped
2 garlic cloves, crushed
200 g (7 oz) pork and fennel sausages,
removed from their casings
finely grated zest of 1 lemon
2 tablespoons shredded sage leaves
45 g (1½ oz/¼ cup) raw unsalted pistachio nuts
large handful parsley, chopped
140 g (5 oz/2 cups) fresh sourdough
breadcrumbs
1 free-range egg, beaten

Preheat the oven to 160°C/320°F (fan-forced).

To make the stuffing, heat the butter and olive oil in a large frying pan over medium heat. Add the onion and garlic and cook for 6–8 minutes, or until the onion is softened. Transfer to a large bowl and set aside to cool, then add the remaining stuffing ingredients and mix well.

Lay the turkey breast, skin side down, on a chopping board. Using a sharp knife, cut horizontally through the thickest part of the breast, nearly to the other side, but not all the way through. Open the fillet out like a book.

Press the stuffing onto the breast, then roll up the turkey to enclose the stuffing. Get someone to help you tie the turkey with kitchen string every 3 cm (1¼ inches) to secure the roll, then place on a roasting rack in a roasting tin. Brush the entire surface of the turkey with the olive oil.

Transfer to the oven and roast for 2 hours, or until the turkey is golden brown, and the juices run clear when you poke a skewer into the centre, or a meat thermometer registers 75°C (167°F) when you test the meat in several places.

Remove the turkey from the oven, cover loosely with foil and leave to rest for 15 minutes. Save the roasting tin juices for making a gravy to serve with the turkey, if desired, or for another use.

Remove and discard the string from the turkey, then carve into slices. Serve scattered with sage, and with gravy and/or cranberry sauce, if desired.

✕ You may need to order a turkey breast roll from your local poultry supplier or butcher. Allow 1 hour of cooking at 180°C/350°F (160°C/320°F fan-forced) for the first 1 kg (2 lb 3 oz) of rolled turkey breast and stuffing, then 20 minutes per 1 kg (2 lb 3 oz) thereafter.

ROAST TURKEY WITH SPICY CRANBERRY SAUCE

SERVES 8–10

1 × 5 kg (11 lb) turkey, fresh or fully thawed
1 teaspoon salt
50 g (1¾ oz) butter, melted

CHORIZO CRANBERRY STUFFING

40 g (1½ oz) butter
2 tablespoons olive oil
2 onions, finely chopped
3 garlic cloves, crushed
½ teaspoon hot smoked paprika (pimentón)
1 fresh chorizo sausage, removed from its casing
500 ml (17 fl oz/2 cups) chicken stock
350 g (12½ oz) thick sourdough bread, torn into
   1.5 cm (½ inch) chunks
120 g (4½ oz/1 cup) roughly chopped pecans
125 g (4½ oz/½ cup) roughly chopped pitted
   prunes
70 g (2½ oz/½ cup) dried cranberries
50 g (1¾ oz/½ cup) finely grated parmesan
large handful parsley, chopped

To make the stuffing, heat the butter and olive oil in a large frying pan over medium heat. Add the onion, garlic, paprika and sausage meat. Cook for 5–8 minutes, or until the onion is softened and the sausage meat cooked through. Transfer to a large bowl and set aside to cool. Add 375 ml (12½ fl oz/1½ cups) of the stock, then the remaining stuffing ingredients. Mix well, then set aside to soak for 10 minutes. (If making ahead, the stuffing can be refrigerated for up to 1 day.)

Preheat the oven to 160°C/320°F (fan-forced). Place a roasting rack in a large roasting tin, and lightly grease a 1.5 litre (51 fl oz/ 6 cup) baking dish.

Tuck the wings under the turkey, sprinkle the salt into the main cavity and tie the legs together with kitchen string. Open up the neck cavity and work your fingertips between the skin and the breast meat, to separate them. Push about 1 cup of the cooled stuffing under the skin, to cover about half of the breast area, to protect it from drying out. Secure the opening with a skewer.

Spoon the remaining stuffing into the greased baking dish, evenly pour the remaining stock over, then cover and refrigerate until required.

Brush the turkey skin all over with the melted butter and season lightly with salt and freshly ground black pepper. Place the turkey on the roasting rack in the roasting tin, then add 500 ml (17 fl oz/ 2 cups) water to the tin. Cover firstly with a large sheet of baking paper, then securely with foil.

Transfer carefully to the oven and roast for 2 hours.

Carefully remove the foil and baking paper. Add the stuffing to the oven and bake the turkey and stuffing for a further 1 hour, or until the stuffing and turkey skin are golden, and the turkey juices run clear when tested with a skewer, inserted into the thickest part of the thigh; a meat thermometer should register 75°C (167°F) when you test the meat in several places.

Remove the turkey from the oven, cover loosely with foil and leave to rest for 30 minutes before carving. Save the roasting tin juices for making a gravy to serve with the turkey, if desired, or for another use.

While the turkey is resting, make the cranberry sauce. Heat the olive oil in a saucepan over medium heat and cook the onion for 5 minutes, or until softened, stirring occasionally. Add the remaining ingredients and bring to the boil, stirring occasionally. Reduce the heat to medium–low and simmer for 10 minutes, or until the fruit is soft, and the sauce has slightly thickened. Season to taste, adding a little more sugar if necessary; sometimes cranberries can be a little bitter. Remove from the heat and set aside to cool.

Carve the turkey and serve with the stuffing and cranberry sauce.

X For every 1 kg (2 lb 3 oz) of turkey, allow 35–40 minutes of cooking time at 160°C/320°F (fan-forced) – about 3 hours for a 5 kg (11 lb) turkey. The cranberry sauce can be made 2–3 days ahead and refrigerated; it yields about 2½ cups.

SPICY CRANBERRY SAUCE

1 tablespoon olive oil

1 onion, finely chopped

500 g (1 lb 2 oz/4½ cups) cranberries, fresh or frozen

2 apples, peeled, cored and chopped

110 g (4 oz/½ cup) brown sugar, approximately

½ teaspoon chilli flakes

80 ml (2½ fl oz/⅓ cup) dry sherry or apple juice

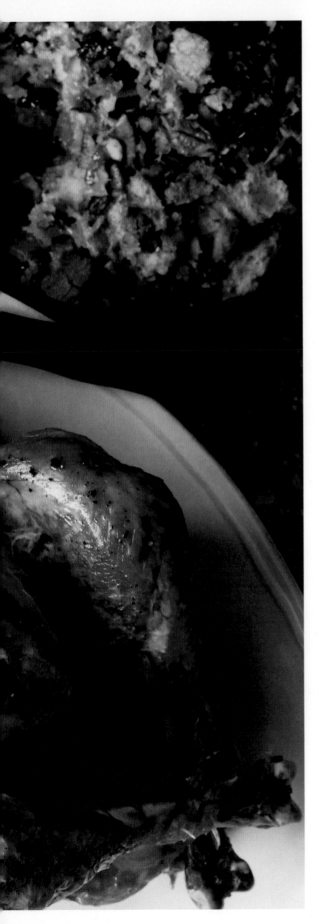

ROAST TURKEY WITH SPICY CRANBERRY SAUCE

✕

DUCK RAGU WITH PASTA

SERVES 4–6

4 duck leg quarters, trimmed of excess fat

2 tablespoons olive oil

2 leeks, white part only, cut in half lengthways,
   then chopped

3 garlic cloves, finely chopped

2 carrots, halved lengthways, then chopped

2 celery stalks, sliced

2 large thyme sprigs

2 rosemary sprigs

2 bay leaves

1 teaspoon fennel seeds, crushed with a knife

375 ml (12½ fl oz/1½ cups) verjuice (see note)
   or white wine

zest and juice of 1 orange

500 ml (17 fl oz/2 cups) chicken stock

chilli flakes (optional)

350 g (12½ oz) short pasta, such as orecchiette

2 generous tablespoons chopped flat-leaf
   (Italian) parsley

Heat a large heavy-based saucepan over medium–high heat.
Season the duck with sea salt flakes and freshly ground black
pepper. Add the duck to the pan, skin side down, and brown for
10 minutes, turning once during cooking. Remove to a plate.

Discard most of the excess fat from the pan, leaving about
2 teaspoons. Add the olive oil and cook the leek, garlic, carrot and
celery over low heat for 5 minutes. Add the herbs and fennel seeds
and cook for a further minute. Return the duck to the pan.

Pour in the verjuice, allow to bubble for a minute or two, then add
the orange zest and juice, stock and a few shakes of chilli flakes,
if using. Bring to the boil, cover the pan, reduce the heat to a low
simmer and cook slowly for 1½ hours.

Remove the lid and simmer on low heat for a further 20 minutes,
you want the liquid to reduce but remain a brothy consistency.
Remove the duck legs, pull the meat from the bones and return it
to the ragu; discard the skin and bones. Discard the thyme sprigs,
rosemary and bay leaves. Season to taste with salt and black pepper.

Meanwhile, bring a large saucepan of water to the boil and cook the
pasta for 10 minutes, or until 'al dente'. Drain and toss with the ragu
and parsley.

✗ Verjuice is made from the juice of unfermented grapes. It adds a
   gentle acidic flavour to dishes.

ROAST DUCK WITH ORANGE & CHERRY SAUCE

SERVES 4

4 duck leg quarters
olive oil, for pan-frying
125 ml (4 fl oz/½ cup) dry sherry
300 g (10½ oz) fresh or frozen cherries, pitted and halved
shredded zest of 1 orange
125 ml (4 fl oz/½ cup) orange juice
1 teaspoon light soy sauce
Lemon & rosemary smashed cannellini beans (page 261) or mashed potato, to serve

Preheat the oven to 160°C/320°F (fan-forced).

Season the duck leg quarters with salt and freshly ground black pepper. Heat a heavy-based flameproof roasting tin over medium heat, then add a splash of olive oil. Cook the duck for 5–6 minutes on each side, or until very well browned all over, using tongs to tilt the legs and brown the sides as well.

Carefully tilt the roasting tin and spoon out any excess fat, saving it for another use (such as roasting potatoes).

Transfer to the oven and roast for 45–50 minutes, or until the duck is tender and the skin is crisp.

Transfer the leg quarters to a plate, cover loosely with foil and leave to rest in a warm place for 15 minutes.

While the duck is resting, make the sauce. Carefully pour the excess fat from the roasting tin, adding it to the previously collected fat. Place the roasting tin back over medium heat and add the sherry, scraping the bottom of the tin to loosen any browned goodness from the duck. Simmer for 2–3 minutes, or until reduced slightly. Add the cherries, orange zest and orange juice and simmer, partially covered, for 10 minutes, or until the cherries are soft and collapsing. Stir in the soy sauce and cook, uncovered, for a further 2–3 minutes, or until slightly thickened. Season to taste.

Serve the duck on a bed of smashed cannellini beans or mashed potato, topped with the cherry sauce.

DUCK & PORK SAUSAGE CASSOULET

SERVES 8

350 g (12½ oz/1¾ cups) dried cannellini beans
1 tablespoon olive oil
200 g (7 oz) piece of pork belly, cut into 2 cm
   (¾ inch) cubes, leaving the skin on
4 duck leg quarters
4 good-quality pork sausages
1 large onion, finely chopped
3 garlic cloves, crushed
1 carrot, cut in half lengthways
2 celery stalks
2 thyme sprigs
2 bay leaves
2 teaspoons sea salt flakes
125 ml (4 fl oz/½ cup) tomato passata
crusty bread, to serve

Place the beans in a large saucepan and cover with 3 litres (101 fl oz/ 12 cups) cold water. Bring to the boil over high heat, then cook for 15 minutes. Remove from the heat and leave the beans to soak for 2 hours in the cooking liquid.

Preheat the oven to 120°C/250°F (fan-forced).

Heat a large flameproof casserole dish over medium heat. Add the olive oil and pork belly cubes. Cook, turning frequently, until the pork is golden and most of the fat has been released. Remove the pork to a bowl and set aside.

Place the duck, skin side down, in the hot casserole dish. Cook for 5 minutes before turning, to achieve a rich, dark crust on the skin. Cook the other side until browned, then remove and leave to rest with the pork.

Brown the sausages in the same dish, turning occasionally, then add to the bowl with the pork and duck. Add the onion, garlic, carrot and celery to the casserole dish. Reduce the heat slightly and cook for 10 minutes, or until the onion is very soft, stirring occasionally to cook evenly. Stir in the thyme sprigs, bay leaves, salt, passata and a generous grind of black pepper.

Return the cooked pork cubes, duck and sausages to the casserole. Drain the beans, then add them to the dish, along with 1.25 litres (42 fl oz/5 cups) water. Transfer the casserole dish to the oven and cook for 3 hours. At this point, a light crust should be forming. Pierce the crust slightly with a fork in about seven places. If the beans are looking dry, add a little extra water down the side of the dish.

Return to the oven and bake for 1– 1½ hours. The cassoulet is ready when a rich, dark crust has formed, the beans are cooked, the mixture looks a little saucy, and the duck is tender and falling from the bone.

Serve in deep bowls, with fresh crusty bread.

ROAST DUCK WITH MAPLE & BALSAMIC GLAZE

Preheat the oven to 170°C/340°F (fan-forced).

Remove the neck from the duck and trim the wings to the second joint. Open the vent at the leg end and drain any liquid from the cavity. Dry the skin with paper towel and season the duck, inside and out, with salt and freshly ground black pepper. Place the lemon halves, sage sprigs and one of the rosemary sprigs in the cavity.

Place the duck on a rack in a roasting tin. Transfer to the oven and roast for 30 minutes.

Meanwhile, make the maple and balsamic glaze. Combine the butter, maple syrup and vinegar in a small saucepan over high heat. Bring to the boil, then reduce the heat and simmer for 5–6 minutes, stirring occasionally, until slightly thickened. Season with salt and freshly ground black pepper.

Tie the remaining three rosemary sprigs together at the woody end with kitchen string, to make a glazing brush. Remove the duck from the oven and brush all over with the glaze, using the rosemary sprigs as a brush. Return the duck to the oven and brush with more glaze every 20 minutes for the next hour, or until cooked through and well glazed, reserving any leftover glaze for the gravy.

Transfer the duck to a warm plate, cover loosely with foil and leave to rest for 20 minutes. While the duck is resting, make a gravy. Pour off most of the duck fat from the roasting tin and save for another use, such as roasting potatoes. Place the roasting tin over medium heat and add the stock. Scrape the base of the pan with a spoon to dislodge all the good bits, then simmer for 5 minutes, or until reduced slightly. In a small bowl, mix the cornflour to a smooth paste with a little water. Add to the stock with any leftover glaze, whisking until combined. Simmer, whisking, for 1–2 minutes, or until slightly thickened. Strain if necessary. Carve the duck and serve with the gravy.

SERVES

1 × 2 kg (4 lb 6 oz) whole duck
1 lemon, cut in half
2 sage sprigs
4 rosemary sprigs
250 ml (8½ fl oz/1 cup) duck or chicken stock
2 teaspoons cornflour (cornstarch)

MAPLE & BALSAMIC GLAZE

60 g (2 oz) butter
125 ml (4 fl oz/½ cup) maple syrup
60 ml (2 fl oz/¼ cup) good-quality balsamic
    vinegar

✕ The approximate roasting time for a whole duck is 40 minutes per 1 kg (2 lb 3 oz).

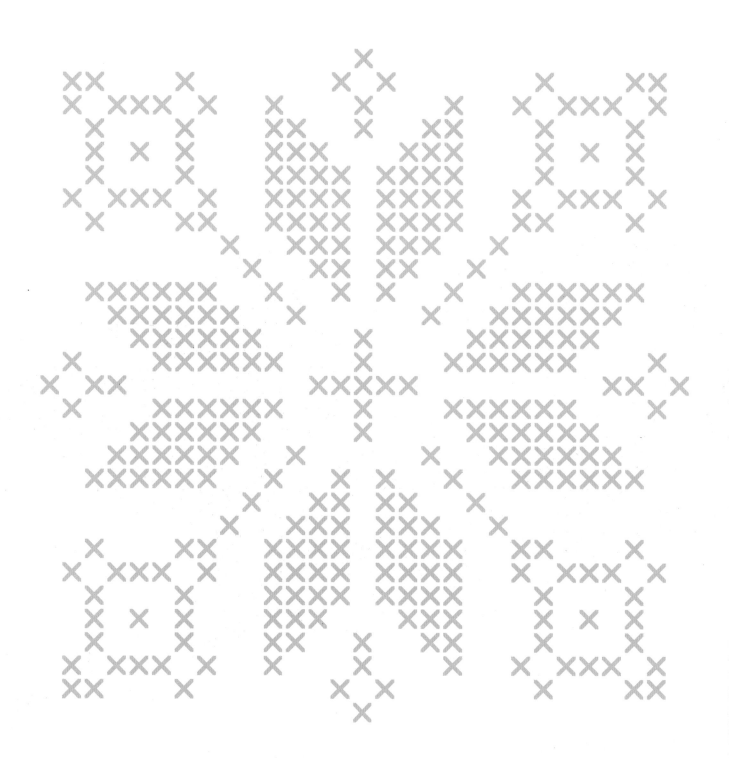

PORK

SLOW-COOKED PORK LASAGNE

SERVES 8

2 tablespoons olive oil
1 large onion, finely chopped
1 large carrot, finely chopped
2 celery stalks, finely chopped
2 garlic cloves, crushed
1 bay leaf
2 rosemary sprigs
2 teaspoons sea salt flakes
1 teaspoon freshly ground black pepper
1 tablespoon balsamic vinegar
125 ml (4 fl oz/½ cup) shiraz or dry red wine
1 kg (2 lb 3 oz) skinless pork belly
400 g (14 oz) tinned crushed tomatoes
500 ml (17 fl oz/2 cups) tomato passata
300 g (10½ oz) fresh lasagne sheets
375 g (13 fl oz/1½ cups) crème fraîche (see note)
60 g (2 oz/½ cup) grated romano cheese
green salad, to serve

Heat the olive oil in a large heavy-based saucepan over medium heat. Add the onion, carrot and celery. Cover and cook for 15 minutes, stirring occasionally, and adding a tablespoon of water if the vegetables catch on the base of the pan. Add the garlic, bay leaf, rosemary, salt and pepper and stir until the garlic is fragrant.

Stir in the vinegar and wine. When the wine is simmering, add the pork and cook for 3 minutes on each side.

Add the tomatoes and passata, stir and cover the pan. Cook over low heat for 2½ hours, stirring occasionally, and adding a little water if the sauce becomes dry.

Preheat the oven to 160°C/320°F (fan-forced).

Remove the pork from the pan. Finely shred the pork using two forks, then stir the shredded pork back into the sauce.

Pour about 375 ml (12½ fl oz/1½ cups) of the sauce into a large baking dish. Then layer the lasagne sheets and sauce into the dish, finishing with the sauce.

In a small bowl, blend the crème fraîche with 2 tablespoons water. Spoon the crème fraîche over the top of the dish and scatter with the cheese.

Bake for 50 minutes, or until the topping is golden brown. Allow to stand for 10 minutes before serving. Serve hot, with a green salad.

✕ In this recipe, crème fraîche is used as a substitute for the more conventional béchamel sauce. You can make your own crème fraîche at home by blending 60 ml (2 fl oz/¼ cup) buttermilk with 340 ml (11½ fl oz/1⅓ cups) thick (double/heavy) cream, and leaving overnight at room temperature before using.

ECUADORIAN SLOW-ROASTED PORK WITH AGRIO SAUCE & SALAD

SERVES 12

juice of 2 limes
juice of 1 grapefruit
60 ml (2 fl oz/¼ cup) olive oil
15 garlic cloves, crushed
1 tablespoon ground cumin
1 tablespoon dried oregano
2 teaspoons sea salt flakes
1 teaspoon freshly ground black pepper
3 kg (6 lb 10 oz) pork leg, skin scored
   (ask your butcher to do this)
2 onions, sliced
500 ml (17 fl oz/2 cups) beer
12 small whole potatoes, scrubbed

AGRIO SAUCE

1 small tomato, finely chopped
1 small red onion, finely chopped
1 long red chilli, finely sliced
25 g (1 oz/½ cup) chopped coriander
   (cilantro) leaves
2 tablespoons grapefruit juice
2 tablespoons orange juice
1 tablespoon lime juice
1 tablespoon lemon juice
1 teaspoon soft brown sugar
½ teaspoon sea salt flakes

SALAD

1 small green cabbage, shredded
50 g (1¾ oz/1 cup, firmly packed) finely
   chopped mint leaves
50 g (1¾ oz/1 cup) chopped coriander
   (cilantro) leaves
½ teaspoon sea salt flakes
juice of 1 lime
1 tablespoon olive oil

In a bowl, combine the lime juice, grapefruit juice, olive oil, garlic, cumin, oregano, salt and pepper. Rub the mixture over the pork leg, working it into the meat, and into the scored lines in the skin. Cover the pork loosely with a clean cloth, allowing air to circulate, and rest the pork overnight in the fridge. Remove from the fridge an hour before cooking.

Preheat the oven to 150°C/300°F (fan-forced).

Spread the onion slices in a deep baking dish, and place a rack in the dish. Lay the pork leg on the rack. Pour the beer into the baking dish. Cover the dish loosely with foil, transfer to the oven and bake for 4 hours.

Remove the foil, add the potatoes to the pan and increase the oven temperature to 180°C/350°F (fan-forced).

Roast for 1¼ hours, or until the potatoes are tender, and the pork skin is crisp. Remove from the oven and allow to rest for 10 minutes.

Meanwhile, combine the agrio sauce ingredients in a bowl and allow to stand at room temperature for 30 minutes before serving.

To make the salad, combine the cabbage, mint and coriander in a large bowl. Dress with the salt, lime juice and olive oil and toss well.

Serve the rested pork with the potatoes, agrio sauce and salad.

ROAST STUFFED PORK WITH APPLES TWO WAYS

SERVES 8

1 x 2 kg (4 lb 6 oz) rolled pork loin
2 tablespoons olive oil, plus extra for brushing
sea salt flakes, for sprinkling
6 granny smith apples

SAGE & APPLE STUFFING

2 Italian-style sausages, about 250 g
   (9 oz) in total
1 tablespoon olive oil
1 onion, diced
1 celery stalk, chopped
2 garlic cloves, crushed
2 granny smith apples, finely diced
1 teaspoon smoked paprika
120 g (4½ oz/1½ cups) fresh breadcrumbs
½ teaspoon salt
½ teaspoon freshly ground black pepper
12 sage leaves, roughly chopped

Untie the rolled loin, place it on a flat surface and use a sharp knife to score the skin. Place the pork on a rack over the sink, skin side up, and pour boiling water over the skin to open up the cuts. Dry with paper towel, then place the pork in the fridge to dry for 3–4 hours, or overnight.

When you're ready to start cooking, remove the pork from the fridge and leave for 30 minutes to bring it to room temperature.

Preheat the oven to 210°C/410°F (fan-forced).

To make the stuffing, remove the sausages from their casings and chop the meat. Heat the olive oil in a frying pan over medium–high heat, then fry the sausage meat until cooked, mashing it with a wooden spoon to break it up. Remove from the frying pan and place in a mixing bowl.

Reduce the heat to medium and add the onion, celery and garlic to the pan. Fry for about 10 minutes, or until soft and translucent, but not browned, then add to the sausage mixture and allow to cool. Add the diced apple, along with the remaining stuffing ingredients, and mix well.

Lay the pork flat, skin side down. Use a sharp knife to partially slice through the thick meaty end of the pork, and gently open it up, so that the loin is now longer and flatter, ready for stuffing. Lay the stuffing evenly over a third of one end of the pork, then tightly roll up the rest of the loin, securing it in place using kitchen string at even intervals down the length of the loin.

Place the pork in a roasting tin. Rub the olive oil over the skin, then season generously with salt flakes. Transfer to the oven and roast for 30 minutes, then reduce the heat to 160°C/320°F (fan-forced) and roast for a further 30 minutes.

Rub the whole apples with a splash of olive oil and season with salt and freshly ground black pepper. Add the apples to the roasting tin and continue to roast for a further 30 minutes. Remove from the oven, cover loosely with foil and set aside to rest for 15–20 minutes before serving.

PORK KNUCKLE WITH APPLE SAUCE & SAUERKRAUT

SERVES 4

4 pork knuckles, preferably pre-brined
   (see method if not)
2 onions, roughly chopped
2 carrots, roughly chopped
2 celery stalks, roughly chopped
4 dried bay leaves
20 black peppercorns
6 dried juniper berries
salt
200 g (7 oz) good-quality sauerkraut

BRINE (OPTIONAL)
salt
5–6 dried juniper berries (optional)

If you are unable to buy brined knuckles, use the following method to prepare the knuckles 2 days ahead of time.

Place the knuckles in a large container that will fit in your fridge, ensuring they can be completely submerged.

To make the brine, measuring as you go, add enough cold water to the container to completely submerge the knuckles. Based on how much water you've used, calculate how much salt you need – every 1 litre (34 fl oz/4 cups) of water will require 155 g (5½ oz/½ cup) of salt. Transfer 600 ml (21½ fl oz) of the water to a saucepan, then add the salt quantity that matches the entire amount of water, along with the juniper berries, if using. Bring to the boil, stirring well to dissolve the salt, then transfer to the fridge to cool completely. When it has cooled, pour the brine back into the container with the knuckles, then cover and leave for up to 2 days, checking now and then to ensure the knuckles stay submerged.

When you're ready to start cooking, drain the knuckles and discard the brine. Using a pair of kitchen scissors, make 1 cm (½ inch) long cuts into the pork skin around the base of the knuckle, about 2 cm (¾ inch) apart.

If you don't have a stockpot large enough to fit all the pork knuckles together, divide the onion, carrot, celery, bay leaves, peppercorns, juniper berries and 2 teaspoons salt between two large saucepans, along with the knuckles. Otherwise, place everythig in the one stockpot. Cover the knuckles with cold water.

Bring to the boil, then reduce the heat to a simmer and cook for 1 hour. Test the knuckles by pushing a meat fork or a sharp knife into the pork – if the meat slides off easily, the knuckles are done. If there is still a little resistance, continue cooking for up to a further 30 minutes.

Remove the knuckles from the liquid and set aside to cool slightly, then pat dry with paper towel. Strain the cooking liquid, reserving half the total liquid.

Preheat the oven to 160°C/320°F (fan-forced).

Use a sharp knife to score the skin around the knuckles. Rub a generous amount of salt into the skin – up to 1½ teaspoons per knuckle.

Set a rack into a roasting tin and place the knuckles on top. Pour 500 ml (17 fl oz/2 cups) of the reserved cooking liquid into the roasting tin. Carefully transfer to the oven. Roast the knuckles for 1 hour, basting every now and then with the remaining reserved liquid.

Use a meat thermometer to check that the internal temperature is above 70°C (160°F). If it isn't, roast the knuckles a little longer, checking every 15 minutes.

Once the internal temperature has reached 70°C (160°F), carefully remove the liquid from the roasting tin.

Return the knuckles to the oven and increase the oven temperature to 210°C/410°F (fan-forced). Roast for a further 30 minutes, or until the skin has turned into crisp crackling.

Remove from the oven, cover loosely with foil and leave to rest for 20 minutes while you make the apple sauce.

To make the apple sauce, place the apple in a small saucepan, along with the sugar, lemon juice and cinnamon, if using. Add 80 ml (2½ fl oz/⅓ cup) water and bring to the boil over medium heat. Reduce the heat to low, then cover and leave to cook for 15–20 minutes, or until the apple has completely broken down. Remove from the heat and mash with a fork, so that you have a chunky sauce.

Gently heat the sauerkraut in a small saucepan until warmed through, then serve with the apple sauce and knuckles.

APPLE SAUCE

575 g (1 lb 4 oz) granny smith apples, peeled, cored and diced
1½ tablespoons sugar
squeeze of lemon juice
pinch of ground cinnamon (optional)

PORK KNUCKLE
WITH APPLE SAUCE
& SAUERKRAUT
✕

HUNGARIAN PORK & BEEF GOULASH

SERVES 6

60 ml (2 fl oz/¼ cup) olive oil
3 onions, chopped
1 red capsicum (bell pepper), finely chopped
1 green capsicum (bell pepper), finely chopped
1 large tomato, chopped
1 tablespoon hot paprika
2 teaspoons sea salt flakes
400 g (14 oz) stewing beef, cut into 3 cm (1¼ inch) chunks
600 g (1 lb 5 oz) pork shoulder, cut into 3 cm (1¼ inch) chunks
25 g (1 oz/¼ cup) sweet paprika
4 potatoes, peeled and cut lengthways into quarters
sourdough bread, to serve

Heat the olive oil in a large heavy-based saucepan over medium heat. Add the onion and cook, stirring, for 10–12 minutes, or until the onion is soft and beginning to turn an even golden colour.

Add the capsicums and tomato and cook, stirring, for a further 2–3 minutes. Stir in the hot paprika and salt, then add the beef and stir to coat with the onion. Cook, stirring, for a few minutes to seal the beef pieces. Now add the pork and cook, stirring, for a further 5 minutes.

Stir in the sweet paprika and 500 ml (17 fl oz/2 cups) boiling water. Cover the pan, reduce the heat to low and simmer, stirring occasionally, for 1 hour.

Add the potato pieces to the pan, pushing them down into the sauce. The liquid should be thickening, but still be saucy; if it is looking a little dry, add another 250 ml (8½ fl oz/1 cup) water. Replace the lid and cook on low for a further 40 minutes.

Serve the goulash in deep bowls, with fresh sourdough bread.

SLOW-COOKED PORK RAGU WITH RIGATONI

SERVES 6

2 tablespoons olive oil
2 red onions, finely chopped
2 garlic cloves, crushed
1 teaspoon chilli flakes
1½ teaspoons sea salt flakes
185 ml (6½ fl oz/¾ cup) dry white wine
2 teaspoons dried basil
2 bay leaves
½ teaspoon soft brown sugar
500 g (1 lb 2 oz) skinless pork belly slices
400 g (14 oz) tinned crushed tomatoes
500 ml (17 fl oz/2 cups) tomato passata
50 g (1¾ oz/1 cup, firmly packed) basil leaves,
    plus extra to garnish
500 g (1 lb 2 oz) rigatoni
shaved parmesan, to serve

Heat the olive oil in a large heavy-based saucepan over medium heat. Add the onion. Cover and cook, stirring occasionally, for 15 minutes, or until very soft and slightly golden; if the onion browns too quickly, add a tablespoon of water.

Add the garlic, chilli flakes and salt and cook, stirring, for 1 minute. Add the wine, dried basil, bay leaves and sugar. When the wine is hot, add the pork. Allow the pork to brown for 1 minute, then turn and cook the other side.

Stir in the tomatoes and passata, and 250 ml (8½ fl oz/1 cup) water. Cover the pan and reduce the heat to low. Cook for 3 hours, checking every 30 minutes to stir and add more water if needed. The sauce should be fairly wet during cooking, but after 3 hours it should have reduced, and become thick and syrupy.

Shred the pork in the pan using two forks. Stir the basil leaves through, to coat them in the sauce.

Fill a large saucepan with water and add 2 teaspoons of salt. Bring to the boil, add the pasta and cook for 10 minutes, or until al dente. Drain the pasta and return to the pot. Add a ladleful of sauce to the pasta and stir it through.

Serve the pasta with the pork ragu, topped with parmesan.

CRISPY PORK BELLY WITH FIVE-SPICE & DIPPING SAUCE

SERVES 4

1 x 1.2–1.4 kg (2 lb 10 oz–3 lb 1 oz) piece
of pork belly, skin scored
(ask your butcher to do this)
1 teaspoon Chinese five-spice
1 tablespoon olive oil
1 tablespoon sea salt flakes
200 g (7 oz) rice stick noodles
2 Lebanese (short) cucumbers, cut
into thin batons
shredded carrot, to serve
coriander (cilantro) sprigs, to serve
mint, to serve
lemon wedges, to serve

HOISIN & GINGER MARINADE

125 ml (4 fl oz/½ cup) hoisin sauce
125 ml (4 fl oz/½ cup) light soy sauce
1 tablespoon grated fresh ginger
1 tablespoon crushed garlic
125 ml (4 fl oz/½ cup) shaoxing rice wine
1 tablespoon brown sugar

CHILLI GINGER DIPPING SAUCE

90 ml (3 fl oz) hoisin sauce
3 garlic cloves, crushed
45 ml (1½ fl oz) light soy sauce
1 tablespoon grated fresh ginger
1 tablespoon honey
1 teaspoon chilli sauce

Place the pork on a roasting rack in the sink, then pour a kettle of boiling water over the skin. Pat dry thoroughly.

To make the marinade, mix the ingredients together in a jug. Place the pork, skin side up, in a shallow dish large enough to lay it out flat. Being careful not to let it touch the skin, pour the marinade around the pork; the marinade is for the flesh only. Carefully transfer to the fridge, and leave to dry, uncovered, for 2–3 hours, or overnight.

When you're ready to start cooking, preheat the oven to 200°C/400°F (fan-forced).

Remove the pork from the marinade and place in a roasting tin. Sprinkle the five-spice, olive oil and salt flakes over the skin and rub it all in, using your hands.

Transfer to the oven and roast for 30 minutes to ensure a crispy crackling, then reduce the oven temperature to 150°C/300°F (fan-forced) and cook for a further 1 hour 20 minutes, or until the pork is tender. If the crackling isn't crisp enough at this point, place the pork under a hot grill (broiler) for a few minutes.

Remove from the oven, cover loosely with foil and leave to rest for 15 minutes.

Just before serving, cook the noodles according to the packet instructions.

To make the dipping sauce, combine the ingredients in a small bowl.

Carve the pork and serve on a nest of noodles, topped with the cucumber, carrot and herbs, with the dipping sauce and lemon wedges alongside.

SMOKY CHIPOTLE BARBECUED PORK RIBS

SERVES 4

4 racks pork baby back ribs, each cut
    in half for easier handling
potato salad, to serve

DRY RUB

3 teaspoons sea salt flakes
3 teaspoons smoked paprika
2 teaspoons soft brown sugar
2 teaspoons dried oregano
1½ teaspoons freshly ground black pepper

SAUCE

1 tablespoon olive oil
2 garlic cloves, crushed
2 cooking apples, peeled, cored and grated
1 teaspoon sea salt
1 teaspoon sweet paprika
2 chipotle chillies in adobo sauce, chopped
250 ml (8½ fl oz/1 cup) tomato passata
60 ml (2 fl oz/¼ cup) maple syrup
2 tablespoons cider vinegar

Preheat the oven to 150°C/300°F (fan-forced).

To make the dry rub, combine the ingredients in a small bowl. Sprinkle evenly over both sides of the pork ribs, pressing it in well.

Wrap the ribs in foil, then place in a single layer on a large baking tray. Transfer to the oven and bake for 2½ hours.

Remove the foil-wrapped ribs from the oven and leave until cool enough to handle.

To make the sauce, heat the olive oil in a small saucepan over low heat and cook the garlic and apple for about 4 minutes, or until soft. Stir in the salt, paprika, chillies, passata, maple syrup and vinegar. Continue to cook over low heat, stirring occasionally, for about 10 minutes, or until the mixture is thick and saucy. Set aside.

Preheat a barbecue grill to medium heat.

Unwrap the ribs, and brush the sauce over both sides. Grill the ribs on both sides, until charred.

Transfer the ribs to a chopping board. Use a sharp knife to cut between the bones.

Pile the ribs onto a serving platter and serve with potato salad.

SLOW-ROASTED PORK SHOULDER WITH ROOT VEGETABLES & APPLE JUS

SERVES 6

1 teaspoon sea salt flakes, plus extra for
   seasoning

½ teaspoon freshly ground black pepper

½ teaspoon soft brown sugar

1 tablespoon lemon juice

2.5 kg (5½ lb) pork shoulder, bone in,
   skin scored

2 apples, cored and sliced into rings

1 red onion, sliced

3 rosemary sprigs

12 baby carrots, scrubbed, leaves trimmed

3 parsnips, peeled and cut in half lengthways

3 turnips, peeled and cut into quarters

Preheat the oven to 130°C/265°F (fan-forced).

In a small bowl, combine the salt, pepper, sugar and lemon juice. Place the pork, skin side down, on a clean board. Rub the seasoning mixture into the meat, taking care to keep the skin clean and dry.

Arrange the apple and onion slices in a baking dish as a base for the pork to rest on. Add the rosemary sprigs and place the pork on top.

Roast for 1 hour to allow the skin to dry out, then cover the dish loosely with foil, reduce the oven temperature to 110°C/230°F (fan-forced) and roast for a further 4 hours.

Remove the baking dish from the oven and remove the foil. Place the vegetables around and under the pork. Baste the vegetables and the meaty sides of the pork with the cooking juices and sprinkle the vegetables and the pork skin with sea salt. Pierce the pork skin with a bamboo skewer in many places.

Increase the oven temperature to 180°C/350°F (fan-forced). Return the dish to the oven to roast, uncovered, for a further 1 hour, or until the vegetables are cooked, the pork is very tender and the pork skin is puffed and crackling.

Transfer the pork, carrots, parsnips and turnips to a warm serving dish.

To make the apple jus, use a spatula to scrape the pan juices, apple and onion fragments from the baking dish into a narrow jug. Scoop the fat off the top, then use a stick mixer to blend the jus.

Transfer the apple jus to a serving jug and serve alongside the roasted pork and vegetables.

PULLED PORK TACOS WITH FRESH PINEAPPLE SALSA

SERVES 8

2 tablespoons olive oil, plus extra
   for charring the pork
1 tablespoon ground cumin
1 tablespoon smoked paprika
2 teaspoons dried oregano
2 teaspoons chilli flakes
2 teaspoons sea salt flakes
3 garlic cloves, crushed
1 tablespoon cider vinegar
3 kg (6 lb 10 oz) pork shoulder, bone in
1 lime, skin on, thickly sliced
1 orange, skin on, thickly sliced
1 red onion, cut into thin wedges

PINEAPPLE SALSA

190 g (6½ oz/1 cup) finely diced fresh
   pineapple
pinch of sea salt flakes
1 red onion, finely chopped
25 g (1 oz/½ cup) chopped coriander
   (cilantro) leaves

TO SERVE

corn tortillas
baby cos (romaine) lettuce leaves
lime wedges

Preheat the oven to 130°C/265°F (fan-forced).

Put the olive oil in a small bowl. Add the cumin, paprika, oregano, chilli, salt, garlic and vinegar and mix to a paste. Spread the paste over the pork.

Place the pork in a baking dish or casserole dish in which it fits snugly. Tuck the lime slices, orange slices and onion wedges around and over the pork. Cover the dish with baking paper, then a sheet of foil, creating a tight seal.

Transfer to the oven and bake for 5 hours. Remove the pork from the oven and unwrap. Leave until cool enough to handle.

When the pork is almost ready, make the pineapple salsa by combining the ingredients in a mixing bowl.

To toast the tortillas before serving, heat a small dry frying pan over high heat. Toast each tortilla for 5–10 seconds on one side only, then wrap in a cloth to keep warm and soft.

Remove the bone from the pork – it should pull out easily. Using tongs, break the meat into large chunks. Heat a large frying pan over high heat and add an extra 2 tablespoons olive oil. Working in batches, taking care not to overcrowd the pan, sear the pork chunks all over, using the tongs to tear the chunks into smaller pieces as they char slightly. Repeat with the remaining pork.

Serve the pork with the pineapple salsa, warm tortillas, lettuce, and lime wedges for squeezing over.

STICKY ROAST PORK RIBS WITH SLAW

SERVES 4

2 large racks of pork ribs, about 2 kg
    (4 lb 6 oz) in total

DRY RUB

55 g (2 oz/¼ cup, firmly packed) soft brown
    sugar
½ teaspoon salt
1 teaspoon cayenne pepper
2 tablespoons smoked paprika
1 tablespoon garlic powder
1 teaspoon mustard powder

BARBECUE SAUCE

230 g (8 oz/1 cup, firmly packed) dark brown
    sugar
4 tablespoons smoked paprika
500 ml (17 fl oz/2 cups) apple cider vinegar
250 ml (8½ fl oz/1 cup) tomato ketchup
90 ml (3 fl oz) worcestershire sauce
1 teaspoon liquid smoke (optional)

SLAW

200 g (7 oz/2⅔ cups) shredded white cabbage
175 g (6 oz/2⅓ cups) shredded red cabbage
1 large carrot, grated
4 spring onions (scallions), finely sliced
120 g (4½ oz) whole-egg mayonnaise
60 g (2 oz/¼ cup) sour cream
1 tablespoon lemon juice
1½ tablespoons pickled jalapeño chillies

Preheat the oven to 130°C/265°F (fan-forced).

To make the dry rub, mix the ingredients together in a small bowl. Using your hands, rub the spices well into the ribs, on all sides. Roll out two double layers of foil on a work surface, and wrap a rack of ribs in each. Crimp the top and sides of the foil so that the parcels are sealed, leaving a few centimetres (about an inch) between the foil and the meat.

Place on a baking tray, transfer to the oven and bake for 2 hours.

While the ribs are cooking, make the barbecue sauce and the slaw.

For the barbecue sauce, place the sugar, paprika, vinegar, ketchup and worcestershire sauce in a small saucepan. Mix until combined, then bring to the boil. Reduce the heat and simmer for about 30 minutes, or until the sauce has reduced by half, and is thick and glossy. Stir in the liquid smoke, if using.

For the slaw, combine all the cabbage, carrot and spring onion in a bowl. In a small bowl, mix together the mayonnaise, sour cream and lemon juice. Put the jalapeños on a chopping board and chop roughly, then use the back of a knife to mash them, so that you end up with a watery paste. Add to the mayonnaise mixture and stir well. Season to taste with salt and plenty of freshly ground black pepper. Toss through the slaw and set aside until ready to serve.

When the 2 hours is up, remove the ribs from the oven and open the foil. Increase the oven temperature to 180°C/350°F (fan-forced). Liberally brush the ribs on all sides with the barbecue sauce, then return to the oven, meat side up, for 10 minutes.

Remove from the oven and brush the meat side again generously with more barbecue sauce, then roast for a further 10 minutes.

Serve the ribs with the slaw, with the remaining barbecue sauce on the side for drizzling and dipping.

MUSTARD-GLAZED ROAST LEG OF HAM WITH PEACH SALSA

SERVES 8–10

115 g (4 oz/½ cup, firmly packed) soft brown
    sugar
125 ml (4 fl oz/½ cup) apple juice
125 ml (4 fl oz/½ cup) maple syrup
2 tablespoons wholegrain mustard
2 tablespoons dijon mustard
1 x 3–4 kg (6 lb 10 oz–8 lb 13 oz) leg of ham,
    skin removed
whole cloves, to decorate

PEACH SALSA

4 peaches, peeled and diced
grated zest and juice of 1 lime
1 fresh jalapeño chilli, seeded and finely diced
½ red onion, diced or finely sliced
3 tablespoons chopped coriander
    (cilantro) leaves
2 tomatoes, diced
1 red capsicum (bell pepper), finely diced

Move an oven rack to the lowest rung, then preheat the oven to 140°C/275°F (fan-forced). Line a large roasting tin with foil or baking paper, and place a roasting rack in the tin.

In a saucepan, combine the sugar, apple juice and maple syrup, stirring over medium heat until the sugar has dissolved. Remove from the heat and stir in the wholegrain and dijon mustards.

Use a sharp knife to score the fat of the ham, in a diamond pattern, taking care not to cut all the way through to the flesh. Stick a clove into the middle of each diamond, then place the ham on the roasting rack in the roasting tin. Baste all over with the maple syrup glaze.

Transfer to the oven and roast for 15 minutes, then baste again with the glaze. Continue to roast for another 1¼ hours, basting at 20-minute intervals.

When the ham is nearly ready, make the salsa by gently mixing all the ingredients together in a bowl.

Remove the ham from the oven and serve with the peach salsa.

ASIAN-STYLE CARAMEL PORK

SERVES 4

1½ tablespoons sunflower, rice bran or
   vegetable oil
1 kg (2 lb 3 oz) pork belly or pork slices,
   cut into 3 cm (1¼ inch) pieces
2 bird's eye chillies, seeds removed (see note),
   finely chopped
6 French shallots, chopped
3 garlic cloves, finely chopped
50 g (1¾ oz/1 bunch) coriander (cilantro),
   stalks finely chopped, leaves reserved
   for garnishing
80 ml (2½ fl oz/⅓ cup) light soy sauce
180 g (6½ oz/1 cup) shaved palm sugar (jaggery)
1 star anise
1 cinnamon stick
2 tablespoons fish sauce
steamed white rice, steamed greens and lime
   wedges, to serve

Heat 2 teaspoons of the oil in a wok until hot. In three batches, brown the pork over high heat, removing each batch to a plate. Drain the pork fat from the wok.

Add the remaining oil to the wok, along with the chilli, shallot, garlic and the coriander stalks. Cook over medium heat for 2 minutes.

Return the pork to the wok. Stir in the soy sauce, sugar, star anise and cinnamon stick and 375 ml (12½ fl oz/1½ cups) water. Reduce the heat to low, cover with a lid and leave to simmer for 1½ hours.

Remove the lid and simmer over low heat for 10 minutes, or until the sauce is syrupy. Stir in the fish sauce.

Garnish with the coriander leaves. Serve with steamed rice and greens, with lime wedges for squeezing over.

✕ If you like a bit of heat, leave the seeds in the chillies.

BRAISED PORK SHOULDER WITH APPLE CIDER & RED CABBAGE

SERVES 6–8

1 kg (2 lb 3 oz) pork shoulder, bone in
1 tablespoon olive oil
150 g (5½ oz) thickly cut smoked streaky bacon,
    cut into 1 cm (½ inch) pieces
2 onions, thinly sliced
2 garlic cloves, crushed
375 ml (12½ fl oz/1½ cups) apple cider
10 juniper berries, crushed
1 small red cabbage, about 1 kg (2 lb 3 oz),
    shredded
60 ml (2 fl oz/¼ cup) cider vinegar
mashed potato, to serve

Preheat the oven to 140°C/275°F (fan-forced).

Season the pork generously with sea salt flakes and freshly ground black pepper. Heat a large flameproof casserole dish over high heat. Add the olive oil and brown the pork well on all sides; this will take 10–15 minutes. Remove the pork from the dish, reduce the heat to medium and cook the bacon until crispy.

Add the onion to the dish and cook, stirring, for 6–8 minutes, or until softened. Add the garlic and cook for 1 minute, until fragrant. Return the pork to the dish and pour over the cider. Add the crushed juniper berries.

Cover the pork with baking paper to reduce evaporation, then put the lid on. Transfer to the oven and bake for 2 hours.

Remove the dish from the oven. Carefully turn the pork over, then place the cabbage around the side of the dish. Pour the vinegar over the cabbage, replace the baking paper and lid, and return to the oven for 1 hour, or until the pork is falling-apart tender.

Using tongs, break the pork into large chunks and remove the bone.

Serve the braised pork and cabbage on a bed of mashed potato, with the pan juices spooned over.

BEEF

BEEF POT ROAST

SERVES 4–6

60 ml (2 fl oz/¼ cup) olive oil
1 × 1–1.4 kg (2 lb 3 oz–3 lb 1 oz) piece of
    beef chuck or blade roast
250 ml (8½ fl oz/1 cup) white wine
500 ml (17 fl oz/2 cups) beef stock
2 thyme sprigs
2 rosemary sprigs
8 new potatoes, scrubbed
8 baby onions, peeled
8–10 baby carrots, peeled and trimmed
crusty bread, to serve

Preheat the oven to 140°C/275°F (fan-forced).

Heat the olive oil in a flameproof casserole dish over medium heat. Brown the beef well, for about 2 minutes on each side, then remove to a plate.

Drain the fat from the casserole dish. Place the beef back in the dish, along with the wine, stock, thyme and rosemary sprigs. Put the lid on, transfer to the oven and cook for 1¼ hours, turning the beef over once during that time.

Remove from the oven, add the potatoes and onions, put the lid back on and bake for 30 minutes.

Add the carrots, then cover and bake for a further 30 minutes.

Remove from the oven and allow the beef to rest for a few minutes before carving.

Serve slices of the beef in bowls, along with the vegetables and a good ladleful of the broth. Enjoy with crusty bread.

SLOW-COOKED BEEF STROGANOFF

SERVES 6

2 tablespoons olive oil, plus an extra
   2 teaspoons
1 kg (2 lb 3 oz) piece of stewing steak
1 onion, thinly sliced
2 garlic cloves, crushed
1 teaspoon sea salt flakes
½ teaspoon freshly ground black pepper
125 ml (4 fl oz/½ cup) tomato passata
2 tablespoons vodka
250 ml (8½ fl oz/1 cup) beef stock
2 tablespoons butter
500 g (1 lb 2 oz) button mushrooms, sliced
125 g (4½ oz/½ cup) crème fraîche or sour cream
3 tablespoons finely chopped flat-leaf
   (Italian) parsley
dill pickles, to serve
Lemon & rosemary smashed cannellini beans
   (page 261) or mashed potato, to serve

Preheat the oven to 130°C/265°F (fan-forced).

Heat 2 tablespoons of the olive oil in a large frying pan over high heat. Brown the beef well on all sides for about 10 minutes, then remove the beef to a casserole dish.

Reduce the heat under the frying pan to medium. Add the onion and cook for 6–8 minutes, or until softened. Add the garlic, salt, pepper and passata and cook, stirring, for another minute. Add the vodka and stock and stir to deglaze the pan. Pour the onion mixture over the beef.

Cover the casserole dish tightly with baking paper, then a sheet of foil, to reduce evaporation. Transfer to the oven and cook for 3 hours, or until the beef is very tender when tested with a fork.

Remove the beef from the casserole and shred roughly using two forks. Return the shredded beef to the casserole dish.

Heat a frying pan over medium heat and add the butter and 2 teaspoons olive oil. When the butter foams, add the mushrooms and cook, stirring occasionally, for about 5 minutes. Remove from the heat, stir in the crème fraîche, then add the mushroom mixture to the casserole and stir it through.

Place the baking paper and foil back on the casserole dish, sealing it tightly. Return to the oven for a further 30 minutes to heat through.

Serve on a bed of smashed cannellini beans or mashed potato, garnished with the parsley and with dill pickles on the side.

STICKY OXTAIL STEW WITH CREAMY POLENTA

SERVES 4

1.3 kg (2 lb 14 oz) oxtail, segmented between
    the bones (ask your butcher to do this for you)
35 g (1¼ oz/¼ cup) plain (all-purpose) flour
about 2 tablespoons olive oil
2 celery stalks, thickly sliced
4 carrots, cut into large chunks
2 garlic cloves, crushed
400 g (14 oz) tinned crushed tomatoes
500 ml (17 fl oz/2 cups) beef stock
125 ml (4 fl oz/½ cup) shiraz or dry red wine
2 bay leaves
1 rosemary sprig
15 g (½ oz/½ cup) finely chopped flat-leaf
    (Italian) parsley

CREAMY POLENTA

1 teaspoon sea salt
150 g (5½ oz/1 cup) polenta
2 tablespoons butter

Preheat the oven to 130°C/265°F (fan-forced).

Season the oxtail pieces generously with sea salt flakes and freshly ground black pepper. Place the flour in a bowl and coat each piece in the flour, shaking off the excess.

In a large flameproof casserole dish, heat the olive oil over medium–high heat. Working in batches, add the oxtail pieces and brown all over; you may need to add a little extra oil. Remove the oxtail to a plate.

Add the celery, carrot and garlic to the pan, along with the tomatoes, stock, wine, bay leaves and rosemary sprig. Cover with a sheet of baking paper and the lid, then transfer to the oven and bake for 2 hours.

Turn the oxtail pieces over, submerging them in the sauce. Replace the baking paper and lid and return to the oven for a further 3 hours.

Remove from the oven and leave until cool enough to handle. Remove the oxtail pieces from the sauce, then pick the meat from the bones. Discard the bones. Skim the fat from the surface of the sauce and return the meat to the pan.

To make the polenta, bring 1 litre (34 fl oz/4 cups) water to the boil in a saucepan over medium–high heat. Add the salt. While stirring gently, pour the polenta into the boiling water in a steady stream. Continue stirring as the polenta thickens. Reduce the heat to low and continue stirring, then cover with a lid and continue cooking for 30 minutes, stirring vigorously every 10 minutes or so, scraping down the sides, bottom and into the corner of the pan. Stir in the butter, then cover and allow to rest for 10 minutes before serving.

Spoon the polenta into deep bowls. Spoon the oxtail stew over, garnish with the parsley and serve.

BOEUF EN CROUTE WITH RED WINE JUS

SERVES 4–6

1 × 750 g (1 lb 11 oz) piece of beef fillet
2 tablespoons olive oil
8–10 slices prosciutto
375 g (13 oz) block or sheet of frozen
   butter puff pastry, thawed
1 free-range egg yolk, beaten
sea salt flakes, for sprinkling

DUXELLES
10 g (¼ oz) dried porcini mushrooms
400 g (14 oz) mixed fresh mushrooms
40 g (1½ oz) butter
2 garlic cloves, crushed
1 French shallot, finely diced
2 large thyme sprigs
80 ml (2½ fl oz/⅓ cup) white wine
1 tablespoon chopped parsley

To prepare the duxelles, put the dried porcini in a small bowl, cover with boiling water and leave to rehydrate for 15 minutes. Clean the fresh mushrooms, place in the bowl of a food processor and chop finely. Set aside.

Heat the butter in a frying pan over medium heat. Sauté the garlic and shallot for 3–4 minutes, or until translucent but not browned. Add the thyme sprigs and chopped fresh mushrooms and cook for 6–8 minutes, or until the mushrooms have darkened and released their juices.

Drain the porcini, reserving 60 ml (2 fl oz/¼ cup) of the soaking liquor. Finely chop the porcini and add to the pan with the white wine then cook for 2–3 minutes. Add the porcini liquor, and leave the mushrooms to cook, stirring frequently, until all the liquid in the pan has disappeared, and you are left with a dark, fragrant, paste-like mixture. This process can take up to 20 minutes – be patient, as the elimination of water will be important for assembling the dish. Remove the thyme stems, stir in the parsley and set aside to cool completely.

Remove the beef from the fridge and leave for 30 minutes to bring it to room temperature. Season well with salt and freshly ground black pepper.

Heat the olive oil in a large frying pan over high heat. Sear the beef on all sides – including both ends – for about 2 minutes on each side. Remove to a plate and allow to cool slightly.

Lay a large piece of plastic wrap, about 60 cm (24 inches) long, on a clean work surface. Lay 4–5 pieces of the prosciutto, slightly overlapping, on the plastic. Layer the remaining prosciutto at the base of the first row of slices, so that you end up with a 'sheet' of prosciutto, large enough to completely encase the beef.

Spread the duxelles evenly over the prosciutto layer, leaving at least 2 cm (¾ inch) free on all edges. Place the beef on top. Lifting the end of the plastic wrap, roll the prosciutto tightly around the beef and duxelles.

Continue to wrap in the plastic, twisting the short edges, so that you end up with a tightly wrapped bundle, with the prosciutto completely encasing the beef and mushroom. Transfer to the fridge and leave to firm up for 10 minutes.

Roll the pastry out to about 40 cm (16 inches) long, and 30 cm (12 inches) across, so that it will be large enough to completely encase the beef. Use the plastic-wrapped parcel to check the size before unwrapping the beef.

Remove the plastic, then lay the prosciutto-wrapped bundle on the pastry. Tightly wrap the pastry around it, folding in the sides. Tightly wrap in another long length of plastic wrap, and return to the fridge again until ready to use; as long as it is well wrapped, the bundle can sit for several hours.

Preheat the oven to 180°C/350°F (fan-forced).

Decorate the pastry as you see fit, then brush with the beaten egg yolk and season with salt flakes. Place in a roasting tin and roast for 35 minutes for rare, or up to 45 minutes for medium-rare, until the pastry is golden brown. Remove from the oven and leave to rest for 10 minutes.

Meanwhile, make the red wine jus. Heat the olive oil over medium-high heat, add the garlic and shallot and cook for 3–4 minutes, stirring constantly. Increase the heat to high and add the thyme sprigs, bay leaf and red wine. Bring to the boil, reduce the heat and leave to simmer for 10 minutes, or until the wine has reduced by about two-thirds. Stir in the stock and continue to simmer for 10–15 minutes, or until the sauce has reduced and is starting to thicken. Strain, place back heat over medium heat and whisk in the butter to give a glossy finish. Transfer to a gravy jug.

Serve the beef in slices with the red wine jus drizzled over.

RED WINE JUS

1 tablespoon olive oil
1 garlic clove, chopped
1 large French shallot, finely diced
3–4 thyme sprigs
1 bay leaf
400 ml (14 fl oz) red wine
350 ml (12 fl oz) beef stock
30 g (1 oz) butter, cubed

BOEUF EN
CROUTE WITH
RED WINE JUS
✕

BEEF
RENDANG

SERVES 4

2 tablespoons peanut or vegetable oil
1 kg (2 lb 3 oz) trimmed stewing steak,
    cut into 3 cm (1¼ inch) cubes
25 g (1 oz/¼ cup) desiccated (shredded)
    coconut
1 lemongrass stem, white part only, bruised
6 kaffir lime leaves
2 cinnamon sticks
1 tablespoon sugar
1 teaspoon sea salt flakes
400 ml (14 fl oz) tinned coconut milk
steamed white rice and steamed greens,
    to serve

SPICE PASTE

6 French shallots, peeled
4 large garlic cloves, peeled
2 lemongrass stems, white part only, chopped
6 bird's eye chillies, seeds removed from
    3 of the chillies
1½ tablespoons finely chopped peeled
    fresh ginger
1½ tablespoons finely chopped peeled
    fresh galangal
1 teaspoon ground coriander
1 teaspoon ground turmeric
2 tablespoons peanut or vegetable oil

To make the spice paste, place all the ingredients in a small food processor. Blend to a chunky paste.

Heat the peanut oil in a large heavy-based saucepan over high heat. Working in three batches, brown the beef well, removing each batch to a plate.

Add the spice paste to the pan and cook, stirring, for 2 minutes. Return the beef to the pan.

In a separate frying pan, lightly toast the coconut for 2 minutes, or until pale golden.

Add the toasted coconut to the beef, along with the lemongrass, lime leaves, cinnamon sticks, sugar and salt. Stir in the coconut milk and 500 ml (17 fl oz/2 cups) water.

Put the lid on and bring to a simmer, then reduce the heat to low. Cook, covered, at a slow simmer for 2½ hours.

Remove the lid. Simmer, uncovered, over low heat for a further 20–30 minutes, or until the curry is quite dry.

Serve with steamed rice and steamed greens.

SLOW-COOKED CUBAN BEEF

SERVES 6

1 kg (2 lb 3 oz) beef skirt steak

olive oil for pan-frying

1 large red onion, sliced

2 small carrots, roughly chopped

2 celery stalks, roughly chopped

3 garlic cloves, lightly crushed

1 bay leaf

400 g (14 oz) tinned crushed tomatoes

1 tablespoon cider vinegar

500 ml (17 fl oz/2 cups) beef stock

2 green capsicums (bell peppers), sliced into 1 cm (½ inch) strips

1 red capsicum (bell pepper), sliced into 1 cm (½ inch) strips

2 tablespoons tomato paste (concentrated purée)

1 teaspoon ground cumin

½ teaspoon dried oregano

125 ml (4 fl oz/½ cup) dry white wine

85 g (3 oz/½ cup) pitted green olives, halved

TO SERVE

cooked white rice

lightly toasted tortillas

Season the beef well with sea salt flakes and freshly ground black pepper. Heat 2 tablespoons olive oil in a large heavy-based saucepan over high heat. Add the beef in a single layer, working in two batches if necessary. Cook for 4 minutes to brown well, then turn and cook for a few minutes to brown the other side. Remove from the pan and set aside.

Add the onion, carrot, celery, garlic and bay leaf to the pan. Cook for 4–5 minutes, then add the tomatoes, vinegar and stock. Stir to scrape the base of the pan, then add the beef back in.

Put the lid on the pan, reduce the heat to low and simmer gently for 2 hours, checking to stir occasionally and top up the liquid with water if necessary.

Heat another 1 tablespoon of olive oil in a large frying pan over medium heat. Add the capsicums and cook, tossing occasionally, for 5 minutes, or until softened. Stir in the tomato paste and fry for a couple of minutes to let the flavour develop. Add the cumin and oregano and cook, stirring, for a minute or two, until the cumin is fragrant.

Deglaze the pan with the wine, then add the capsicum mixture to the beef. Leave to simmer for 30 minutes.

Remove the beef from the saucepan and pull it into shreds, using two forks. Mix the beef back into the braise, along with the olives. Simmer for a final 5 minutes.

Allow to stand for 10 minutes, before serving with cooked rice and warm tortillas.

BEEF & PORK MEATLOAF WITH BUTTERMILK MASH

SERVES 6–8

2 free-range eggs
1 tablespoon buttermilk
1 tablespoon cider vinegar
1 teaspoon honey
1½ teaspoons sea salt flakes
½ teaspoon freshly ground black pepper
2 teaspoons smoked paprika
2 teaspoons sweet paprika
500 g (1 lb 2 oz) minced (ground) beef
500 g (1 lb 2 oz) minced (ground) pork
3 garlic cloves, crushed
1 red onion, finely diced
1 carrot, grated
15 g (½ oz/½ cup) finely chopped flat-leaf
    (Italian) parsley
45 g (1½ oz/¾ cup) panko breadcrumbs
olive oil, for brushing
steamed green beans, to serve

BUTTERMILK MASH

1 kg (2 lb 3 oz) mashing potatoes, peeled
    and cut into large chunks
500 g (1 lb 2 oz) sweet potatoes, peeled
    and cut into large chunks
1 teaspoon sea salt flakes
1 tablespoon butter
250 ml (8½ fl oz/1 cup) buttermilk

SMOKY GLAZE

250 g (9 oz) cherry tomatoes
1 small onion, quartered
3 garlic cloves, unpeeled
1 tinned chipotle chilli in adobo sauce
3 tablespoons soft brown sugar
¼ teaspoon sea salt flakes

Fill a baking dish with water and place on the lowest shelf of the oven. Preheat the oven to 160°C/320°F (fan-forced).

Whisk the eggs, buttermilk, vinegar, honey, salt, pepper and smoked and sweet paprika together in a large bowl. Add the beef, pork, garlic, onion, carrot, parsley and breadcrumbs and mix well.

Brush a rectangular baking dish with olive oil. Form the meat mixture into a loaf shape in the dish, then brush the loaf with 2 teaspoons olive oil. Place in the oven and bake for 20 minutes.

Reduce the oven temperature to 140°C/275°F (fan-forced). Bake the meatloaf for a further 90 minutes, topping up the water in the baking dish as needed.

Meanwhile, make the buttermilk mash. Place the potatoes and sweet potatoes in a saucepan and just cover with cold water. Add the salt and bring to the boil, then reduce the heat to low and simmer for about 30 minutes, or until tender. Drain the water and add the butter. Mash the potatoes. Warm the buttermilk in a small saucepan, then add to the potatoes, season with freshly ground black pepper and stir in until well blended. Keep warm.

To make the smoky glaze, heat a frying pan over high heat and add the tomatoes, onion and garlic. Cook, turning frequently, until the vegetables and garlic are charred. Cool slightly, peel the garlic, then place in a blender with the tomatoes, onion and chilli. Blend until smooth. Wipe out the pan and return the blended tomato mixture to the pan with the sugar and salt. Cook over medium heat for 4–5 minutes, or until slightly thickened, stirring occasionally.

Serve the meatloaf in slices on a bed of buttermilk mash, topped with the smoky glaze and some green beans on the side.

BEEF CHEEKS BAKED IN RED WINE

SERVES 4

2 tablespoons plain (all-purpose) flour
4 beef cheeks, about 800 g (1 lb 12 oz) in total
2 tablespoons olive oil
2 onions, cut into chunks
6 garlic cloves, sliced
1 large carrot, thickly sliced
2 celery stalks, thickly sliced
3 rosemary sprigs
3 sage sprigs
2 tablespoons tomato paste (concentrated purée)
500 ml (17 fl oz/2 cups) red wine
350 ml (12 fl oz) beef stock
mashed potato, to serve
steamed green beans, to serve

Preheat the oven to 130°C/265°F (fan-forced).

Put the flour in a zip-lock bag and season well with salt and freshly ground black pepper. Toss the beef cheeks in the flour, ensuring they are coated evenly, then shake off the excess.

Heat the olive oil in a flameproof casserole dish over medium–high heat. Working in batches if necessary, brown the cheeks well, for about 2 minutes on each side. Remove and set aside.

Reduce the heat to medium, add the onion, garlic, carrot and celery to the pan and fry for 4–5 minutes, or until the vegetables have softened. Add the rosemary, sage and tomato paste, stir to combine, then cook for a further 1–2 minutes.

Pour in the wine, stirring well to loosen any bits that have stuck to the bottom of the dish. Allow the wine to come to the boil, then simmer for 3–4 minutes. Stir in the stock, bring back to the boil, then turn off the heat.

Return the beef cheeks to the dish, pushing them down so they are covered by the sauce. Put the lid on, then transfer to the oven to bake for 2½–3 hours, turning the cheeks once or twice so they cook evenly.

Serve on a bed of mashed potato and with green beans on the side.

OSSO BUCCO WITH GREMOLATA

SERVES 4

50 g (1¾ oz) butter
2 celery stalks, finely diced
2 carrots, finely diced
2 onions, finely diced
2 tablespoons tomato paste (concentrated purée)
2 garlic cloves, crushed
2 lemon rind strips, all white pith removed
2 tablespoons olive oil
35 g (1¼ oz/¼ cup) plain (all-purpose) flour
8 veal osso bucco, about 1.5 kg (3 lb 5 oz) in total (see note)
250 ml (8½ fl oz/1 cup) dry white wine
400 g (14 oz) tinned crushed tomatoes
250 ml (8½ fl oz/1 cup) beef stock or water
2 bay leaves
1 thyme sprig
soft polenta or mashed potato, to serve

GREMOLATA

1 anchovy fillet
1 small garlic clove, peeled
3 tablespoons coarsely chopped flat-leaf (Italian) parsley
2 teaspoons grated lemon zest

Preheat the oven to 140°C/275°F (fan-forced).

Heat the butter in a large heavy-based flameproof casserole dish with a tight-fitting lid. Cook the celery, carrot and onion over medium heat, stirring occasionally, for 10 minutes, or until softened. Add the tomato paste and cook for a further 2 minutes. Add the garlic and lemon rind, stir until fragrant, then remove from the heat.

In a large frying pan, heat the olive oil over medium–high heat. Toss the veal in the flour, shaking off the excess. Fry the veal, in batches if necessary, for 6–8 minutes, until well browned on both sides. Place the veal in the casserole dish, in a single layer on top of the vegetables.

Drain most of the fat from the frying pan. Add the wine to the frying pan and simmer for 2 minutes, scraping up any bits stuck to the base of the pan. Pour the mixture over the veal, along with the tomatoes and stock; the veal should be just covered in liquid, so add a little more stock or water if necessary. Add the bay leaves and thyme. Return the casserole to the heat and bring to the boil.

Put the lid on, transfer to the oven and cook for 1½–2 hours, or until the veal is tender. It should be falling from the bone, but still holding its shape. If the cooking liquid is a little thin at this point, carefully transfer the veal to a plate and cover with foil to keep warm. Return the casserole to the stovetop and boil the sauce until thickened to the desired consistency. Return the veal to the casserole to coat in the sauce.

Meanwhile, to make the the gremolata, finely chop the anchovy and garlic together. Combine in a small bowl with the parsley and lemon zest.

Serve the osso bucco and sauce scattered with the gremolata, with your choice of accompaniment.

✗ If veal is unavailable, use beef osso bucco. It is likely to be larger in size, so may also take a little longer to cook.

BARBECUED
BEEF BRISKET

For the dry rub, combine the ingredients in a small bowl, mixing well. Rub the mixture all over the beef. At this point you can wrap the beef in plastic wrap and cure it overnight in the refrigerator, or continue with the recipe.

To make the barbecue sauce, heat the olive oil in a frying pan and cook the onion, celery and garlic for 5 minutes, until softened, stirring often. Add the stock and simmer for about 10 minutes, or until reduced by half. Leave to cool slightly, then transfer the mixture to a blender. Add the remaining barbecue sauce ingredients and blend until smooth.

Mix half the barbecue sauce with 500 ml (17 fl oz/2 cups) water. Place the beef in a shallow roasting tin and pour the sauce mixture around the sides. Cover tightly with baking paper, then a sheet of foil.

Set up a charcoal grill for indirect grilling and preheat it to low. You will need to cover the grill while cooking. Put the roasting tin in place, pull the lid down and cook the beef for 5–6 hours, or until the meat is very tender.

Increase the heat in the barbecue grill to medium–high.

Remove the brisket from the roasting tin and place on the grill to char. Cover with the lid and cook for about 20 minutes, turning the meat carefully, until lightly charred all over. Remove the beef from the heat, then cover and leave to rest for 15 minutes.

Meanwhile, pour the roasting juices into a small saucepan, stir in the remaining barbecue sauce and cook over medium–low heat until syrupy.

Slice the rested beef across the grain. Transfer to a serving platter and pour the barbecue sauce over. Serve as part of a buffet meal, or with coleslaw and fresh white buns.

SERVES 12

3 kg (6 lb 10 oz) beef brisket, with fat cap intact
coleslaw, to serve
fresh white bread buns, to serve

DRY RUB
1 tablespoon chilli powder
1 teaspoon ground cumin
1 teaspoon mustard powder
2 teaspoons soft brown sugar
1 tablespoon sea salt flakes
1 teaspoon freshly ground black pepper

BARBECUE SAUCE
1 tablespoon olive oil
1 small red onion, finely chopped
1 stalk celery, chopped
2 garlic cloves, crushed
250 ml (8½ fl oz/1 cup) beef stock
200 ml (7 fl oz) tomato ketchup
50 ml (1¾ fl oz) worcestershire sauce
1 tablespoon cider vinegar
2 teaspoons hot English mustard
2 teaspoons smoked paprika

✗ Instead of cooking the brisket using a charcoal grill, you can bake it in a preheated 140°C/275°F (fan-forced) oven for the same length of time, then char it in a large grill pan or frying pan.

BEEF, STOUT & BLACK PEPPER STEW

SERVES 6–8

1.5 kg (3 lb 5 oz) oyster blade steak, diced

35 g (1¼ oz/¼ cup) plain (all-purpose) flour

60 ml (2 fl oz/¼ cup) olive oil

2 carrots, roughly chopped

2 onions, sliced

3 garlic cloves, sliced

2 tablespoons tomato paste (concentrated purée)

375 ml (12½ fl oz/1½ cups) stout

250 ml (8½ fl oz/1 cup) beef stock

2 teaspoons freshly ground black pepper

pinch of sea salt flakes

mashed potato, to serve

steamed greens, to serve

Toss the beef in the flour, shaking off the excess. Heat the olive oil in a large heavy-based saucepan over medium–high heat. Brown the beef in batches, then return all the meat and any juices to the pan.

Add the carrot, onion and garlic. Stir in the tomato paste, stout, stock, pepper and salt. Stir well and bring to the boil. Put the lid on, then reduce the heat to low and simmer for 1¼ hours, or until the beef is almost tender.

Remove the lid and cook, uncovered, for a further 30 minutes, or until the beef is very tender but still holding its shape, and the sauce is slightly thickened.

Serve with mashed potato and steamed greens.

✕ This stew can also be cooked in the oven. Prepare the stew in a large flameproof casserole dish that has a tight-fitting lid. When the stock and stout have been added to the stew, and it has come to the boil on the stovetop, put the lid on and cook in a preheated 140°C/275°F (fan-forced) oven for 1½–2 hours, or until the beef is tender.

CHIPOTLE & CHORIZO CHILLI CON CARNE

SERVES 4

2 tablespoons olive oil
1 red onion, finely chopped
2 garlic cloves, crushed
1 fresh Mexican chorizo sausage,
    skin removed
1 teaspoon ground cumin
1 teaspoon smoked paprika
1 tinned chipotle chilli in adobo sauce,
    chopped
1 bay leaf
400 g (14 oz) tinned crushed tomatoes
125 ml (4 fl oz/½ cup) beef stock
500 g (1 lb 2 oz) stewing steak, cut into
    large cubes
110 g (4 oz/½ cup) dried black beans, rinsed
juice of 1 lime
2 squares dark chocolate
1 handful coriander (cilantro) leaves and
    stems, chopped, plus extra leaves, to serve
1 tomato, chopped
1 avocado, chopped
cooked white rice, to serve

Heat the olive oil in a large heavy-based saucepan over medium heat. Add the onion and garlic and cook for 3 minutes, or until softened. Crumble the chorizo into the pan, add the cumin and paprika and cook, stirring, for 2–3 minutes, until the chorizo is cooked.

Stir in the chipotle chilli, bay leaf, tomatoes and stock and bring to a simmer. Stir in the beef, then cover the pan and cook over low heat for 30 minutes.

Add the beans, lime juice, chocolate, coriander and 500 ml (17 fl oz/2 cups) water. Cover and continue to cook for a further 1½ hours, stirring occasionally, and adding more water if necessary. The consistency should be thick but not too dry. Season to taste with sea salt flakes and freshly ground black pepper.

Serve topped with tomato, avocado and coriander leaves, with a side of cooked white rice.

STICKY FIVE-SPICE BEEF RIBS

SERVES 4

1.5 kg (3 lb 5 oz) beef short ribs
110 g (4 oz/½ cup, firmly packed) soft brown
    sugar
1 tablespoon chinkiang black vinegar, malt
    vinegar or rice vinegar
coriander (cilantro) leaves, to garnish

MARINADE

125 ml (4 fl oz/½ cup) dark soy sauce
125 ml (4 fl oz/½ cup) light soy sauce
165 g (6 oz/¾ cup, firmly packed) soft brown
    sugar
4 garlic cloves, crushed
4 cm (1½ inch) piece of fresh ginger, peeled
    and finely grated or chopped
½ teaspoon sea salt flakes
1 red chilli, finely chopped

FIVE-SPICE POWDER

1 cinnamon stick
1 star anise
½ teaspoon fennel seeds
½ teaspoon whole cloves
½ teaspoon sichuan peppercorns

PICKLED CUCUMBER

125 ml (4 fl oz/½ cup) rice vinegar
55 g (2 oz/¼ cup) sugar
1½ teaspoons salt
2 Lebanese (short) cucumbers, sliced
    lengthways, seeds removed, then
    thinly sliced

Combine the marinade ingredients in a shallow bowl.

Put the five-spice powder ingredients in a small food processor or spice grinder. Blend to a fine powder, then add to the marinade, mixing well.

Add the ribs to the marinade, coating well on all sides. Cover and leave to marinate for 1 hour.

Preheat the oven to 120°C/250°F (fan-forced).

In a heavy-based saucepan, flameproof casserole or cast-iron dish, brown the ribs over high heat, in batches if necessary. Reduce the heat, then return all the ribs to the pan, along with the marinade and 500 ml (17 fl oz/2 cups) water.

Put the lid on, then transfer to the oven and cook for 3¼ hours, or until the ribs are very tender and the meat is falling from the bone.

Meanwhile, make the pickled cucumber. Combine the vinegar, sugar and salt in a small saucepan. Pour in 125 ml (4 fl oz/½ cup) water and stir over medium heat to dissolve the sugar. Bring to a simmer. Place the cucumbers in a heatproof ceramic or glass bowl and pour the liquid over. Gently press on the cucumbers to keep them submerged. Allow to cool for 1 hour, then cover and chill completely in the fridge. Drain just before using.

When the ribs are done, remove them from the sauce, to a platter; cover and leave to rest. Stir the brown sugar and vinegar into the sauce and simmer for 15 minutes, or until syrupy.

Spoon the sticky sauce over the ribs. Garnish with coriander and serve with the pickled cucumber.

X The pickled cucumber will keep in an airtight container in the fridge for up to a week.

ROAST BEEF RIBS WITH PARSNIPS & HORSERADISH CREAM

SERVES 6

2 onions, roughly chopped
2 carrots, roughly chopped
2.3–2.5 kg (5 lb–5½ lb) rack of beef ribs
  (3–4 'points' or bones)
3–4 parsnips, peeled and cut into pieces
Yorkshire puddings (page 249), to serve

HERB & SALT CRUST

1 tablespoon black peppercorns
2 teaspoons rock salt
1 teaspoon garlic salt
1 tablespoon chopped parsley
1 tablespoon chopped rosemary
60 ml (2 fl oz/¼ cup) olive oil

HORSERADISH CREAM

60 g (2 oz/¼ cup) prepared horseradish
  (from a jar)
125 ml (4 fl oz/½ cup) thickened cream,
  whipped
90 g (3 oz/⅓ cup) sour cream
1 teaspoon chopped chives (optional)

Preheat the oven to 200°C/400°F (fan-forced).

For the herb and salt crust, use a mortar and pestle to roughly bash the peppercorns and rock salt for a few seconds, so they are broken down slightly, but still quite coarse. Transfer to a small bowl and add the garlic salt, parsley, rosemary and olive oil, stirring to combine.

Arrange the onion and carrot in a roasting tin and place the beef ribs on top, bone side down. Rub the salt crust mixture onto the beef, making sure all sides are well coated. Add the parsnip around the beef.

Transfer to the oven and roast for 15 minutes. Reduce the oven temperature to 160°C/320°F (fan-forced), and continue to roast to your preferred doneness – for rare, 15 minutes per 450 g (1 lb); for medium, 20 minutes per 450 g (1 lb); for well done, 25 minutes per 450 g (1 lb). Use a meat thermometer if in doubt – 60°C (140°F) for rare, 65–70°C (149–158°F) for medium, and 70–75°C (158–167°F) for well done.

Transfer the beef and vegetables to a plate, cover loosely with foil and a dish towel, and leave to rest for 20 minutes, while you make the horseradish cream.

Combine the horseradish cream ingredients in a bowl. Season to taste with salt and freshly ground black pepper, mixing well.

Carve the beef and serve with the vegetables, horseradish cream and Yorkshire puddings.

LAMB & GAME

MIDDLE EASTERN LEG OF LAMB WITH COUSCOUS SALAD

SERVES 4–6

2 onions, sliced into thick rings
1 x 2 kg (4 lb 6 oz) lamb leg, bone in

MARINADE
zest and juice of 1 lemon
60 ml (2 fl oz/¼ cup) pomegranate syrup
3 garlic cloves, crushed
1 teaspoon ground cumin
1 teaspoon sea salt flakes
½ teaspoon ground cinnamon
½ teaspoon sweet paprika

COUSCOUS SALAD
185 g (6½ oz/1 cup) couscous
½ teaspoon sea salt flakes
½ teaspoon ground cumin
250 ml (8½ fl oz/1 cup) boiling water
400 g (14 oz) tinned chickpeas, rinsed
    and drained
3 spring onions (scallions), thinly sliced
15 g (½ oz/½ cup) finely chopped flat-leaf
    (Italian) parsley
25 g (1 oz/½ cup) chopped mint leaves
1 Lebanese (short) cucumber, finely diced
seeds from ½ pomegranate
80 g (2¾ oz/½ cup) raw almonds, chopped
50 g (1¾ oz/⅓ cup) crumbled feta
1 tablespoon olive oil
juice of 1 lemon

Preheat the oven to 140°C/275°F (fan-forced).

Arrange the onion slices in a roasting dish and place the lamb leg on top.

In a small bowl, mix the marinade ingredients together until well combined, then pour over the lamb. Pour 125 ml (4 fl oz/½ cup) water into the base of the roasting dish. Cover tightly with baking paper, then a sheet of foil. Transfer to the oven and cook for 3 hours.

Remove the foil and paper. Baste the lamb with the pan juices, then roast for a further 30 minutes to brown. Remove from the oven and rest for 15 minutes before carving.

To make the salad, put the couscous in a mixing bowl with the salt and cumin. Pour the boiling water over and cover the bowl tightly with plastic wrap. Rest for 5 minutes, then fluff the couscous grains with a fork and allow to cool. Add the chickpeas, spring onion, parsley, mint, cucumber, pomegranate seeds, almonds and feta. Drizzle with the olive oil and lemon juice, and toss to combine well. Leave at room temperature until the lamb has rested.

Carve the lamb and arrange on a platter. Pour a spoonful of pan juices over the meat and serve with the couscous salad.

LAMB VINDALOO CURRY WITH CUCUMBER SALAD

SERVES 4

1 kg (2 lb 3 oz) boneless lamb shoulder,
  cut into 3 cm (1¼ inch) cubes
1 tablespoon peanut oil
1 onion, finely chopped
3 small dried red chillies
1 cinnamon stick
1 bay leaf
1 cardamom pod
½ teaspoon ground turmeric
1 teaspoon soft brown sugar
1 teaspoon sea salt flakes
½ teaspoon freshly ground black pepper
steamed white rice, to serve

MARINADE

1 teaspoon cumin seeds
1 teaspoon black mustard seeds
1 teaspoon fenugreek seeds
2 teaspoons coriander seeds
3 garlic cloves, crushed
3 cm (1¼ inch) piece of fresh ginger,
  peeled and grated
1 tablespoon apple cider vinegar
1 tablespoon peanut oil

CUCUMBER SALAD

5 Lebanese (short) cucumbers
1 teaspoon sea salt
250 g (9 oz/1 cup) plain yoghurt
2 teaspoons lemon juice
1 garlic clove, crushed
1 tablespoon finely chopped mint leaves

Start by making the marinade. Heat a small dry frying pan over medium heat. Add the cumin, mustard, fenugreek and coriander seeds and toast for a minute, or until fragrant. Grind the seeds using a mortar and pestle, then tip into a mixing bowl. Add the garlic, ginger, vinegar and peanut oil and stir to blend well.

Add the lamb to the marinade, stirring until well coated. Cover and marinate in the fridge for 2 hours.

Heat the peanut oil in a saucepan over medium heat. Add the onion and cook, stirring, for about 5 minutes, or until softened and turning golden brown.

Add the marinated lamb, along with the chillies. Cook, turning occasionally, to brown the lamb on all sides. Add the cinnamon stick, bay leaf, cardamom pod, turmeric, sugar, salt and pepper. Pour in 500 ml (17 fl oz/2 cups) water, stirring to mix the spices through.

Bring to the boil, reduce the heat, then cover and simmer for 1½ hours, or until the lamb is tender.

Meanwhile, prepare the salad. Leaving the skin on, cut the cucumbers in half lengthways and remove the seeds. Slice thinly into half-rounds and place in a mixing bowl. Sprinkle with the salt and toss well, then transfer to a colander and leave to drain for 20 minutes.

Combine the yoghurt, lemon, garlic and mint in a bowl, add the drained cucumber and mix well.

Serve the curry over steamed rice, with the cucumber salad on the side.

LAMB SHANKS WITH CANNELLINI BEANS

SERVES 4

2 tablespoons plain (all-purpose) flour
4 lamb shanks
2 tablespoons olive oil
2 onions, diced
3 garlic cloves, crushed
1 chorizo sausage, diced
2 rosemary sprigs
1 tablespoon smoked paprika
250 ml (8½ fl oz/1 cup) pale ale
250 ml (8½ fl oz/1 cup) beef stock
600 g (1 lb 5 oz) chopped tinned tomatoes
2 × 400 g (14 oz) tins cannellini beans,
    drained and rinsed

BABY SPINACH SALAD

200 g (7 oz) baby English spinach
¼ red onion, finely sliced
3 teaspoons olive oil
1 teaspoon balsamic vinegar

Preheat the oven to 140°C/275°F (fan-forced).

Put the flour in a large zip-lock bag and season well with salt and freshly ground black pepper. Toss the lamb shanks, one at a time, in the bag, until evenly coated with flour. Set aside.

Heat the olive oil in a flameproof casserole dish over medium heat. Working with two at a time, brown the shanks well for about 2 minutes on each side, then remove to a plate.

Add the onion, garlic and chorizo to the casserole dish and fry for 4–5 minutes, or until softened. Add the rosemary, paprika, beer, stock and tomatoes, stirring well. Season with more salt and pepper, bring to the boil, then remove from the heat.

Return the shanks to the dish, put the lid on and transfer to the oven. Cook for 1½ hours, turning the shanks once.

Stir in the beans and cook for a further 20 minutes.

To make the salad, toss the spinach and red onion together, then drizzle with the olive oil and vinegar.

Serve the shanks with the salad on the side.

MOROCCAN LAMB STEW

SERVES 4–6

600 g (1 lb 5 oz) boneless lamb shoulder,
   cut into 5 cm (2 inch) chunks
1 tablespoon olive oil
2 onions, chopped
1 red capsicum (bell pepper), sliced
3 large tomatoes, roughly chopped
1 sweet potato, peeled and cut into large chunks
1 tablespoon honey
45 g (1½ oz/¼ cup) dried apricots
1½ teaspoons sea salt flakes
2 bay leaves
400 g (14 oz) tinned chickpeas, rinsed
   and drained
plain yoghurt, to serve
coriander (cilantro) leaves, to garnish

MARINADE

1 tablespoon sweet paprika
1 tablespoon ground turmeric
1 teaspoon ground cinnamon
1 teaspoon ground cumin
½ teaspoon freshly ground black pepper
2 garlic cloves, crushed
3 cm (1¼ inch) piece of fresh ginger,
   peeled and grated
1 tablespoon olive oil
1 tablespoon cider vinegar

To make the marinade, combine the ingredients in a mixing bowl and stir to blend well. Add the lamb and mix well to coat it in the spices. Cover and allow to marinate at room temperature for 30 minutes.

Preheat the oven to 130°C/265°F (fan-forced).

Heat the olive oil in a flameproof casserole dish over medium heat. Working in two batches, brown the lamb all over, then remove to a plate.

Reduce the heat to medium and cook the onion and capsicum for 5 minutes, stirring occasionally. Return the lamb and any juices to the dish. Add the tomatoes, sweet potato, honey, apricots, salt and bay leaves. Pour in 375 ml (12½ fl oz/1½ cups) water, stirring to mix the spices through. Put the lid on, transfer to the oven and bake for 1½ hours.

Stir the chickpeas into the stew, adding a little water if it looks a bit dry. Replace the lid and bake for a further 1½ hours, or until the lamb is very tender.

Serve the stew in deep bowls, topped with a dollop of yoghurt and coriander leaves.

SLOW-ROASTED GREEK LAMB SHOULDER

SERVES 6

60 ml (2 fl oz/¼ cup) olive oil
6 boiling potatoes, such as desiree,
    Dutch cream, kipfler (fingerling) or
    pink eye, scrubbed and thinly sliced
1 onion, thinly sliced
6 garlic cloves, skin on, smashed
6 rosemary sprigs
2 bay leaves
1 lemon, sliced, plus extra wedges to serve
1 tablespoon dried Greek oregano
1 lamb shoulder, about 2 kg (4 lb 6 oz),
    jointed by your butcher
500 ml (17 fl oz/2 cups) lamb stock, chicken
    stock or water
40 g (1½ oz) butter, softened

Preheat the oven to 140°C/275°F (fan-forced).

Drizzle 2 tablespoons of the olive oil into a deep roasting dish. Add the potato and onion slices, tossing to coat them with the oil and spreading them around the pan. Sprinkle with sea salt flakes and freshly ground black pepper.

Arrange three garlic cloves, three rosemary sprigs, one of the bay leaves and half the lemon slices over the potatoes to form a bed for the lamb. Sprinkle with half the oregano.

Heat the remaining oil in a large non-stick frying pan over high heat. Sprinkle the lamb well with sea salt and cook for 4–5 minutes on each side, or until well browned. Place in the roasting dish and scatter with the remaining garlic, herbs and lemon slices.

Pour most of the fat from the frying pan. Add the stock to the pan and cook over medium heat, scraping up all the tasty bits from the bottom of the pan. Carefully pour the mixture into the roasting dish.

Dot the butter evenly over the lamb and potatoes. Cover the dish with baking paper, then seal with foil. Transfer to the oven and roast for 3½–4 hours, or until the lamb is very tender.

Remove the roasting dish from the oven. Increase the oven temperature to 180°C/350°F (fan-forced).

Remove the foil and baking paper from the dish. Carefully pour off the juices for a delicious sauce, skimming off the fat when it has had a chance to settle. Return the roasting dish to the oven and roast the lamb for a further 10–15 minutes, or until well browned.

Transfer the lamb to a plate, cover loosely with foil and leave to rest for 20 minutes before serving.

Meanwhile, return the potatoes to the oven again to allow the top layer to become crispy. Serve the lamb with the potatoes, pan juices and extra lemon wedges.

ASIAN-STYLE STICKY LAMB RIBS

SERVES 4

2 × 800 g (1 lb 12 oz) racks of lamb ribs
3 garlic cloves, crushed
2 tablespoons grated fresh ginger
1 long red chilli, finely chopped
60 ml (2 fl oz/¼ cup) kecap manis (see note)
2 tablespoons oyster sauce
2 tablespoons dark soy sauce
2 tablespoons palm sugar (jaggery)
1 teaspoon sesame oil
juice of 2 limes
2 lemongrass stalks
2 star anise
steamed jasmine rice, to serve
steamed bok choy, to serve
4 spring onions (scallions), sliced finely
1 tablespoon sesame seeds, toasted

Preheat the oven to 130°C/265°F (fan-forced).

Find a baking dish large enough to hold both racks of lamb; each lamb rack can be cut in half, if required, to fit your baking dish.

In a small bowl, combine the garlic, ginger, chilli, kecap manis, oyster sauce, soy sauce, palm sugar, sesame oil and lime juice. Brush the mixture over the lamb, then transfer the lamb to the baking dish.

Discard the dry leafy tops from the lemongrass stalks. Bruise the white stem of each one with the back of a knife, then cut each lemongrass stem into three pieces. Add to the baking dish with the star anise.

Cover the dish tightly with baking paper and a sheet of foil. Transfer to the oven and bake for 2 hours. Carefully remove the paper and foil, then turn the ribs over. Seal up tightly again, then bake for a further 1 hour.

Remove the lamb from the oven. Leave to cool slightly, then use a sharp knife to cut the lamb into segments between the ribs.

Serve on steamed rice and bok choy, sprinkled with the spring onion and toasted sesame seeds.

✕ Kecap manis is a dark, thick, sweet Indonesian soy sauce, available from Asian grocery stores.

RED WINE & ROSEMARY LAMB SHANKS WITH CAULIFLOWER PURÉE

SERVES 4

35 g (1¼ oz/¼ cup) plain (all-purpose) flour
1 teaspoon sea salt flakes
1 teaspoon freshly ground black pepper
4 French-trimmed lamb shanks
2 tablespoons olive oil, approximately
1 onion, finely diced
1 carrot, finely diced
2 celery stalks, finely diced
2 garlic cloves, crushed
4 rosemary sprigs
1 teaspoon soft brown sugar
250 ml (8½ fl oz/1 cup) shiraz or dry red wine
2 tablespoons balsamic vinegar
250 ml (8½ fl oz/1 cup) tomato passata
zest and juice of 1 orange
steamed green beans, to serve

CAULIFLOWER PURÉE

½ cauliflower, broken into florets
2 tablespoons sour cream
½ teaspoon sea salt flakes
pinch of freshly ground black pepper

Preheat the oven to 130°C/265°F (fan-forced).

Place the flour in a shallow dish, mixing the salt and pepper through. Add the lamb shanks and toss to coat, shaking off any excess flour.

Heat a large flameproof casserole dish over high heat. Add the olive oil and brown the lamb shanks all over, then remove to a plate.

Reduce the heat to medium and cook the onion, carrot and celery for 2 minutes, stirring and adding a little more oil if required. Add the garlic and rosemary and cook for a further minute.

Add the sugar, wine, vinegar, passata, orange zest and juice, and 250 ml (8½ fl oz/1 cup) water. Stir well, scraping up any bits sticking to the bottom of the dish. Return the shanks and any juices to the dish.

Cover with baking paper and put the lid on. Transfer to the oven and bake for 2 hours. Stir the mixture, turn the shanks over, then cover and bake for a further 2 hours, or until the meat is very tender.

To make the cauliflower purée, bring a saucepan of water to the boil over high heat. Add the cauliflower and cook for 10 minutes, or until tender. Drain, then add the sour cream, salt and pepper. Allow to cool slightly, then transfer to a blender and purée until smooth.

Serve the lamb shanks and sauce on the cauliflower purée with steamed green beans on the side.

WEST INDIAN LAMB CURRY WITH COCONUT RICE

SERVES 4–6

2 tablespoons mild curry powder
2 teaspoons sea salt flakes
½ teaspoon freshly ground black pepper
2 garlic cloves, crushed
4 cm (1½ inch) piece of fresh ginger,
    peeled and grated
juice of 1 lime
800 g (1 lb 12 oz) boneless lamb shoulder,
    cut into large chunks
60 ml (2 fl oz/¼ cup) peanut oil
1 onion, roughly chopped
500 ml (17 fl oz/2 cups) vegetable stock
6 allspice berries
1–2 small hot red chillies
1 small green capsicum (bell pepper), sliced
1 small red capsicum (bell pepper), sliced
2 spring onions (scallions), sliced
3 tablespoons chopped coriander (cilantro)
    leaves and stems, plus extra leaves to garnish
1 sweet potato, peeled and cut into 4 chunks
1 potato, peeled and quartered

COCONUT RICE
400 g (14 oz/2 cups) long-grain white rice
250 ml (8½ fl oz/1 cup) coconut milk

Combine the curry powder, salt, pepper, garlic, ginger and lime juice in a mixing bowl. Add the lamb and toss to coat well in the spices. Cover and marinate in the fridge for 2 hours.

Heat the peanut oil in a large heavy-based saucepan over high heat. Add the lamb and stir to coat it in the oil. Put the lid on, reduce the heat to low and cook for 30 minutes.

Add the onion and cook, stirring, for 6–8 minutes, or until softened. Stir in 250 ml (8½ fl oz/1 cup) of the stock, add the allspice berries, then cover and cook for a further 1 hour.

Stir in the chillies, capsicums, spring onion, coriander and remaining stock. Cover and continue to simmer over low heat for a further 1 hour.

Add the sweet potato and potato, and a little water if the curry is dry. Cover and simmer for a further 30 minutes.

To make the coconut rice, place the rice, coconut milk and 500 ml (17 fl oz/2 cups) water in a saucepan. Bring to the boil over medium heat, reduce the heat to low, then cover and simmer for 10 minutes. Stand, covered, for 10 minutes before serving.

Serve the curry and coconut rice in deep dishes, garnished with the extra coriander leaves.

SLOW-ROASTED LAMB LEG WITH POTATOES

SERVES 6

1 leg of lamb, weighing about 2 kg (4 lb 6 oz)

1 small bunch oregano

5 garlic cloves, peeled and sliced in half lengthways

2 tablespoons olive oil

125 ml (4 fl oz/½ cup) white wine

1 lemon, quartered

800 g (1 lb 12 oz) Dutch cream or other roasting potatoes, scrubbed and cut into wedges

185 g (6½ oz/1 cup) unpitted kalamata olives

1 tablespoon chopped parsley

150 g (5½ oz/1 cup) crumbled feta

1 teaspoon sea salt flakes

Preheat the oven to 200°C/400°F (fan-forced).

Use a small sharp knife to cut 10 evenly distributed holes into the lamb. Into each hole, stuff 2–3 oregano leaves and half a garlic clove; this should use up about half the oregano. Rub the olive oil over the lamb and generously season with salt and freshly ground black pepper.

Place the lamb in a large roasting tin, transfer to the oven and roast for 25 minutes.

Remove the roasting tin from the oven, pour in the wine and 190 ml (6½ fl oz/¾ cup) water, then cover the tin tightly with foil. Reduce the oven temperature to 140°C/275°F (fan-forced) and cook the lamb for a further 1 hour.

Add the lemon, potatoes and olives to the roasting tin. Cover again with the foil and bake for a further 1¼ hours.

Remove the foil, increase the oven temperature to 190°C/375°F (fan-forced), and leave to roast for a final 20 minutes.

Remove the lamb from the roasting tin, cover loosely with foil and set aside to rest.

Meanwhile, return the roasting tin to the oven, and roast the potatoes, uncovered, for an additional 20 minutes, so they start to brown.

In a small bowl, mix together the parsley, feta and salt flakes.

Transfer the lamb to a large serving dish and arrange the potatoes, olives and lemon quarters alongside. Skim off the fat from the roasting tin juices, then drizzle the juices over the lamb. Sprinkle the feta mixture over the potatoes and serve.

MINI LAMB ROASTS WITH CHIMICHURRI

SERVES 4

2 mini lamb roasts, about 350 g (12½ oz) each
olive oil, for drizzling
400 g (14 oz) cherry tomatoes, on the vine

CHIMICHURRI
60 g (2 oz/2 cups, firmly packed) parsley
5–6 garlic cloves, roughly chopped
¼ red onion, roughly chopped
17 g (½ oz/⅔ cup, firmly packed) fresh
   oregano leaves
80 ml (2½ fl oz/⅓ cup) red wine vinegar
¾ teaspoon chilli flakes
½ teaspoon salt
¼ teaspoon freshly ground black pepper
270 ml (9 fl oz) olive oil

Preheat the oven to 200°C/400°F (fan-forced).

Season the lamb well with salt and freshly ground black pepper. Place in a roasting tin and top with a drizzle of olive oil.

Transfer to the oven and roast for 20 minutes for rare, 25–30 minutes for medium, or 35 minutes for well done.

Remove from the oven, cover loosely with foil, and leave to rest for 10 minutes.

While the lamb is resting, toss the tomatoes in a splash of olive oil, season with salt and pepper, place on a baking tray and roast for 10 minutes.

To make the chimichurri, combine all the ingredients in the small bowl of a food processor, and whiz until the herbs and onion are finely chopped.

Carve the lamb and serve with the tomatoes and chimichurri.

MOUSSAKA

SERVES 8–10

2 red capsicums (bell peppers)
2 tablespoons olive oil, plus extra for brushing
2 onions, finely chopped
2 garlic cloves, crushed
2 bay leaves
2 cinnamon sticks
500 g (1 lb 2 oz) minced (ground) lamb
500 g (1 lb 2 oz) minced (ground) veal
2 teaspoons sea salt flakes
2 teaspoons dried oregano
1 teaspoon ground cumin
800 g (1 lb 12 oz) tinned crushed tomatoes
1 tablespoon cider vinegar
4 small eggplants (aubergines), cut into
    ½ cm (¼ inch) slices
ground cinnamon, for dusting

BÉCHAMEL SAUCE

100 g (3½ oz) butter
75 g (2¼ oz/½ cup) plain (all-purpose) flour
750 ml (25½ fl oz/3 cups) whole milk
½ teaspoon sea salt flakes
⅛ teaspoon ground nutmeg
⅛ teaspoon ground cloves
100 g (3½ oz) grated kefalograviera, or another
    hard salty sheep's cheese such as Pecorino
    Romano, parmesan or kefalotyri

Preheat the oven to 200°C/400°F (fan-forced).

Place the whole capsicums on an oven rack and roast for 20 minutes, or until the skins are blackened. Remove the capsicums to a small bowl, cover and allow to cool. When cool enough to handle, discard the capsicum stalks, skin, ribs and seeds. Finely chop the flesh and set aside.

Heat 2 tablespoons olive oil in a large saucepan over medium heat. Add the onion, garlic, bay leaves and cinnamon sticks and cook, stirring occasionally, for about 6 minutes. Add the lamb and cook until browned, stirring to break up the lumps. Add the veal and continue to cook, stirring, until browned. Stir in the salt, oregano, cumin and roasted capsicum and cook for 5 minutes, stirring occasionally.

Stir in the tomatoes and vinegar. Put the lid on, reduce the heat to a simmer and cook for 40 minutes, adding a little water if needed. While the sauce is simmering, heat a large grill pan or frying pan over high heat. Brush the eggplant slices with olive oil and cook for a few minutes on each side, or until well browned. Dust the warm eggplant slices with a light dusting of cinnamon and set aside.

To make the béchamel sauce, melt the butter in a saucepan over low heat. Stir in the flour and cook, stirring, for 1–2 minutes. Add the milk, one-third at a time, stirring between additions until smooth. Stir in the salt, nutmeg and cloves, then simmer over low heat, stirring occasionally, for 10 minutes. Remove from the heat and stir in the cheese.

Preheat the oven to 160°C/320°F (fan-forced). To assemble the moussaka, place one-third of the eggplant slices in the base of a lightly greased baking dish. Spread half the tomato sauce mixture over the top. Add half the remaining eggplant slices, then top with the remaining tomato sauce mixture. Layer the remaining eggplant slices over the top, then cover with the béchamel sauce.

Bake for 1 hour, or until golden brown on top. Remove from the oven and allow to stand for 15 minutes before serving, for the moussaka to firm up.

CINNAMON LAMB CASSEROLE WITH RISONI

SERVES 4

2 tablespoons olive oil

600 g (1 lb 5 oz) boneless lamb shoulder,
   cut into 3 cm (1¼ inch) chunks

1 onion, diced

1 eggplant (aubergine), roughly chopped

3 garlic cloves, crushed

2 cinnamon sticks

1 large strip of lemon peel

4 oregano sprigs

3 thyme sprigs

2 bay leaves

1½ teaspoons sea salt flakes

½ teaspoon freshly ground black pepper

500 ml (17 fl oz/2 cups) chicken stock

400 g (14 oz) tinned crushed tomatoes

juice of 1 lemon

100 g (3½ oz/½ cup) risoni

fresh green salad, to serve

Preheat the oven to 140°C/275°F (fan-forced).

Heat the olive oil in a large heavy-based saucepan over high heat.

Working in batches, brown the lamb evenly all over, then transfer to a low-sided casserole or baking dish.

Reduce the heat under the saucepan to low and cook the onion, stirring, for 4–5 minutes, or until softened. Add the eggplant, garlic, cinnamon sticks, lemon peel, herbs, salt and pepper. Cook, stirring, for a further 2–3 minutes, then deglaze the pan with 250 ml (8½ fl oz/1 cup) of the stock, releasing any bits stuck to the bottom. Pour the mixture over the lamb.

Stir in the tomatoes and remaining stock. Cover the dish tightly with baking paper and a sheet of foil, then transfer to the oven and bake for 2 hours.

Remove the paper and foil. Stir in the lemon juice and risoni, adding a little water if necessary. Bake for a further 30 minutes, or until the pasta is cooked.

Remove from the oven and allow the casserole to stand for 10 minutes before serving.

SLOW-ROASTED RABBIT STEW

SERVES 6

1 × 700 g (1 lb 9 oz) rabbit
50 g (1¾ oz/⅓ cup) plain (all-purpose) flour
60 ml (2 fl oz/¼ cup) olive oil
200 g (7 oz) pancetta, cut into batons
2 carrots, finely chopped
1 celery stalk, finely chopped
1 onion, finely chopped
2 garlic cloves, crushed
1 rosemary sprig
1 sage sprig
190 ml (6½ fl oz/¾ cup) red wine
400 g (14 oz) tin chopped tomatoes
375 ml (12½ fl oz/1½ cups) vegetable stock
   or water
2 roasted red capsicums (bell peppers),
   cut into strips
80 g (2¾ oz/½ cup) cracked large green olives
handful parsley

Preheat the oven to 140°C/275°F (fan-forced).

Rinse the rabbit and pat dry with paper towel. Chop the rabbit into pieces, as though you are cutting up a whole chicken: cut off the hind legs (which can also be cut in half again) and the front legs; cut the rib cage away and discard; cut the saddle into four pieces.

Put the flour in a large zip-lock bag and season with salt and freshly ground black pepper. Add the rabbit pieces and shake to dust them in the flour. Shake off the excess flour.

In a flameproof casserole dish with a tight-fitting lid, heat the olive oil over medium–high heat. Working in batches if necessary, sear the rabbit pieces all over for several minutes, or until golden. Transfer to a plate and set aside.

Add the pancetta to the casserole dish and cook for 5 minutes, or until lightly browned. Reduce the heat to medium–low, add the carrot, celery and onion and cook, stirring occasionally, for 10 minutes, or until the vegetables are soft. Add the garlic and the herb sprigs and cook for 2–3 minutes, or until fragrant.

Return the rabbit to the dish, add the wine and cook for 2 minutes, scraping the bottom of the dish to dislodge the lovely browned bits. Stir in the tomatoes and stock and bring to the boil.

Put the lid on, transfer to the oven and bake for 1 hour. Stir in the capsicum, mixing well. Put the lid back on and bake for a further 30 minutes, or until the meat just begins to fall off the bones. Stir in the olives and parsley and serve.

SIDE DISHES

THYME & SUMAC HASSELBACK POTATOES

Preheat the oven to 180°C/350°F (fan-forced). Line a baking tray with foil.

Lay one potato on a chopping board, and place two wooden spoons or two large chopsticks along the length of either side of the potato. Starting at one end and working to the other, cut thin slices into the potato,, bringing the knife down to the wooden spoons, which will prevent you cutting all the way through. This will take some time, but the effect will be worth your patience. Repeat with the remaining potatoes.

Gently fan out the potatoes, to allow the fat to get between the slices, then place on the baking tray.

Melt about 1 tablespoon of the butter, and mix with the olive oil, thyme, rosemary and sumac. Brush the butter mixture onto the potatoes, using the bristles to gently get some of the butter between the slices. Season with salt and freshly ground black pepper.

Transfer to the oven and roast for 30 minutes. Melt the remaining butter, use it to baste the potatoes, then roast for a further 15 minutes.

Season with salt and pepper, garnish with extra thyme and serve.

SERVES 4

8 medium-sized roasting potatoes
60 g (2 oz) butter
2 tablespoons olive oil
1 teaspoon thyme leaves, plus extra to garnish
1 teaspoon chopped rosemary leaves
1 teaspoon sumac

YORKSHIRE PUDDINGS

MAKES 12

80 ml (2½ fl oz/⅓ cup) beef dripping or
    sunflower oil
250 g (9 oz/1⅔ cups) plain (all-purpose) flour
200 ml (7 fl oz) full-cream (whole) milk
110 ml (4 fl oz) cold water
4 free-range eggs, beaten
pinch of salt

Move an oven rack to the upper shelf, then preheat the oven to
210°C/410°F (fan-forced).

Drizzle the dripping into the cups of a 12-hole muffin tin, dividing
it equally. Transfer to the oven and leave to heat for 10 minutes, or
until smoking.

Meanwhile, mix together the remaining ingredients in a bowl until
you have a smooth batter. Set aside until the dripping has heated.

Carefully remove the muffin tin from the oven. Working carefully, as
the fat will be very hot, divide the batter among the 12 muffin holes.

Place back in the oven and bake for 25–30 minutes, without
opening the oven, until the puddings are golden brown and puffed
up. Serve immediately.

MAPLE-ROASTED PUMPKIN

SERVES 4

60 ml (2 fl oz/¼ cup) olive oil
1 butternut pumpkin (squash)
60 ml (2 fl oz/¼ cup) maple syrup
50 g (1¾ oz/½ cup) pecans, chopped

Preheat the oven to 160°C/320°F (fan-forced). Pour half the olive oil into a roasting tin and place it in the oven to heat up.

Peel the pumpkin and slice into rounds, 2 cm (¾ inch) thick. Cut the slices in half and remove the seeds and stringy flesh.

Remove the roasting tin from the oven and carefully add the pumpkin in a single layer. Season with salt and freshly ground black pepper and return to the oven for 10–15 minutes, turning occasionally.

Meanwhile, combine the remaining olive oil and the maple syrup in a small screw-top jar. Season with salt and freshly ground black pepper and add the chopped pecans. Pop the lid on and give the jar a good shake.

Pour the dressing over the pumpkin and roast for a further 10–15 minutes, turning occasionally to stop the dressing sticking to the base of the tin, until the pumpkin is soft and cooked through and the pecans are caramelised.

Transfer to a serving dish and serve immediately.

BACON-WRAPPED STUFFED ONIONS

Preheat the oven to 180°C/350°F (fan-forced).

Cut the tops and bottoms from the onions, so that they sit flat on a chopping board, then peel them. Working with one onion at a time, make a perpendicular slit through the first two outer layers of the onion. Use your fingers to gently prise the layers open, enough so that the inner layers of the onion can be pushed out, leaving you with a hollow round. Dice the inner layers of two of the onions, and set aside; save the remaining onion inners for another use.

Place the hollowed-out onions in a bowl of cold water and leave to soak while you make the stuffing.

Heat the olive oil in a frying pan and fry the sausage meat over medium heat until cooked through, mashing with a wooden spoon as it cooks to ensure there are no large pieces of meat. Remove from the pan with a slotted spoon, into a bowl.

Add the diced onion and celery to the pan. Reduce the heat to medium–low and cook for 4–5 minutes, or until softened, but not browned.

Add the onion and celery to the sausage meat, along with the herbs and breadcrumbs. Season well with salt and freshly ground black pepper. Add the melted butter and stock, then stir to combine.

Drain the onions. Lay one on a flat surface, and use your hands or a small spoon to stuff the onion cavity with the sausage mixture until full, ensuring the stuffing is firmly packed. Wrap a slice of bacon around the onion, then secure with a toothpick. Repeat with the remaining onions, stuffing mixture and bacon.

Transfer to the oven and roast for 20 minutes, or until the bacon is golden brown.

Serve hot, removing the toothpicks just before serving.

MAKES 6

6 small–medium sized onions
1 tablespoon olive oil
2 pork sausages, removed from their
    casings and chopped
1 celery stalk, finely sliced
1½ teaspoons thyme leaves
1½ teaspoons chopped sage
100 g (3½ oz/1¼ cups) fresh breadcrumbs
20 g (¾ oz) butter, melted
80 ml (2½ fl oz/⅓ cup) chicken stock
6 slices streaky bacon

ASPARAGUS BUNDLES WRAPPED IN PROSCIUTTO

Preheat the oven to 180°C/350°F (fan-forced). Line a baking tray with baking paper.

To make the dressing, whisk together the lemon juice, mustard and 60 ml (2 fl oz/¼ cup) of the olive oil. Season with salt and freshly ground black pepper and set aside.

Trim the woody ends from the asparagus, and toss the spears with the remaining olive oil, massaging the oil in to ensure each spear is coated. Season with salt and pepper.

Arrange the asparagus into four bundles, with 5–6 spears in each. Tightly wrap a slice of prosciutto around each bundle, and place on the baking tray, seam side down.

Transfer to the oven and roast for 10–12 minutes, or until the prosciutto begins to crisp and the spears are just tender.

Transfer to a serving dish, drizzle some dressing over each bundle, top with the parmesan and serve.

SERVES 4

2 tablespoons lemon juice
2 teaspoons dijon mustard
75 ml (2½ fl oz) olive oil
20–24 asparagus spears
4 slices prosciutto
small handful shaved parmesan

JALAPEÑO THREE-CHEESE CAULIFLOWER

SERVES 4–6

1 cauliflower, stalk removed, cut into
   large florets
75 g (2¾ oz) butter
75 g (2¾ oz/½ cup) plain (all-purpose) flour
560 ml (19 fl oz/2¼ cups) full-cream
   (whole) milk
65 g (2¼ oz) cheddar, grated
65 g (2¼ oz) red leicester, grated
65 g (2¼ oz) mozzarella, grated
3 tablespoons chopped pickled jalapeño chillies
60 g (2 oz/¾ cup) fresh breadcrumbs

Preheat the oven to 160°C/320°F (fan-forced).

Cook the cauliflower florets in a large saucepan of salted boiling water, until almost tender when tested with a sharp knife. Drain and set aside.

To make the cheese sauce, melt 45 g (1½ oz) of the butter in a saucepan over medium heat. Add the flour and cook, stirring, for 3–4 minutes. Using a spoon or whisk, stir in about 170 ml (5½ fl oz/⅔ cup) of the milk, ensuring there are no lumps. When fully combined, stir in the rest of the milk. Bring to the boil, reduce the heat to low and simmer for 2–3 minutes.

Add 50 g (1¾ oz) each of the cheddar, leicester and mozzarella. Stir well to combine, until all the cheese has melted and the sauce has thickened. Remove from the heat and stir in the jalapeño chillies.

Arrange the cauliflower in a baking dish in a single layer, then pour the cheese sauce over.

Combine the breadcrumbs and remaining cheese in a bowl. Melt the remaining butter, drizzle over the breadcrumb mixture and mix well. Scatter the mixture over the cauliflower.

Transfer to the oven and bake for 40 minutes, or until the topping is golden and the cheese sauce is bubbling. Remove from the oven and serve.

ROASTED RED CABBAGE WITH DRIED FIG GLAZE

SERVES 4–6

100 g (3½ oz) dried figs, finely chopped
2 tablespoons red wine vinegar
125 ml (4 fl oz/½ cup) Pedro Ximénez, or
    other good-quality sweet sherry
a few rosemary sprigs, leaves picked
½ red cabbage, chopped into 4–6 wedges
2 garlic cloves, finely chopped
125 ml (4 fl oz/½ cup) olive oil

To make the glaze, combine the figs, vinegar, sherry, rosemary and 60 ml (2 fl oz/¼ cup) water in a small saucepan then season with salt and freshly ground black pepper. Cook over medium heat for 10–12 minutes, or until the liquid has reduced into a syrup. Set aside.

Meanwhile, preheat the oven to 160°C/320°F (fan-forced). Line a large baking tray with foil.

Place the cabbage wedges on the baking tray. Sprinkle with the garlic, drizzle with the olive oil and season with salt and pepper. Roast for 10–15 minutes, or until the edges are starting to crisp.

Turn the cabbage wedges over and spoon the fig glaze over. Return to the oven and roast for a further 10–15 minutes, or until the cabbage is cooked through and the glaze is bubbling.

Serve warm.

LEMON & ROSEMARY SMASHED CANNELLINI BEANS

SERVES 4

1 tablespoon olive oil

1 onion, finely diced

2 garlic cloves, crushed

2 × 400 g (14 oz) tins cannellini beans,
    drained and rinsed

60 ml (2 fl oz/¼ cup) chicken stock

2 tablespoons crème fraîche

1 tablespoon lemon juice

lemon zest, to garnish

¾ teaspoon finely chopped rosemary,
    plus extra to garnish

Heat the olive oil in a saucepan over medium heat. Add the onion and garlic and fry gently for 3–4 minutes, or until the onion is soft and translucent, but not browned.

Add the beans and stock and bring to the boil. Simmer for 3–4 minutes, or until the beans are fully warmed through.

Remove from the heat and add the crème fraîche, lemon juice and rosemary. Use a potato masher to mash the beans, until they are semi-smooth.

Serve warm, garnished with lemon zest and extra rosemary.

ROAST SMASHED POTATOES

SERVES 4

1 kg (2 lb 3 oz) Dutch cream or other roasting
  potatoes, peeled and cut into evenly
  sized chunks
3 tablespoons duck fat
2 rosemary sprigs
8 garlic cloves, unpeeled
sea salt flakes, for sprinkling

Preheat the oven to 180°C/350°F (fan-forced).

Bring the potatoes to the boil in a saucepan of salted water. Reduce the heat and leave to simmer for 5–6 minutes. Drain in a colander, and return to the saucepan. Leave for 5 minutes to allow the excess moisture to evaporate, then cover the pan and give it a really good shake, so that the edges of the potatoes get roughed up.

Put the duck fat in a large roasting tin, transfer to the oven and leave for 5 minutes to heat up. Carefully remove from the oven and add the potatoes, taking care as the hot fat may splatter.

Toss the potatoes to ensure they are evenly coated in the fat, then return to the oven. Roast for 30 minutes, untouched.

Remove the roasting tin from the oven. Turn the potatoes over, gently pressing down on each using a potato masher, to squish them slightly. Add the rosemary and garlic and roast for a further 20–30 minutes, or until the potato edges are crispy and golden brown.

Serve hot, topped with the roasted garlic and the rosemary sprigs, and sprinkled with a generous amount of sea salt flakes.

BRUSSELS SPROUTS WITH CANNELLINI BEANS & CRUMBLED PANCETTA

SERVES 4

100 g (3½ oz) sliced pancetta

300 g (10½ oz) brussels sprouts, trimmed and cut in half

1 tablespoon olive oil

30 g (1 oz) butter, cubed

400 g (14 oz) tin cannellini beans, drained and rinsed

125 ml (4 fl oz/½ cup) chicken stock

2 tablespoons grated parmesan

lemon wedges, to serve

Preheat the oven to 180°C/350°F (fan-forced). Line a baking tray with baking paper.

Place the pancetta on the baking paper and roast for 4–5 minutes, or until crisp. Remove from the oven, leave to cool, then break into pieces. Set aside and keep warm.

Remove the baking paper, then arrange the brussels sprouts on the baking tray. Add the olive oil, season with salt and freshly ground black pepper and toss well. Dot the cubed butter over the sprouts, then roast for 15–20 minutes, or until slightly charred, turning them over halfway through.

While the sprouts are in the oven, put the beans in a small saucepan with the stock over low heat. Bring to the boil, then simmer gently for 10 minutes, or until warmed through.

Using a slotted spoon, remove the beans from the stock and put them into a serving dish. Toss with the parmesan. Scatter the brussels sprouts over, and crumble the pancetta over the top. Serve warm, with the lemon wedges.

CAULIFLOWER & CELERIAC MASH WITH SAGE BURNT BUTTER

Place the cauliflower and celeriac in a saucepan of boiling water. Bring to the boil, then reduce the heat and simmer for 15 minutes, or until the vegetables are tender. Drain.

Transfer the vegetables to a food processor and blend for a few seconds, until mostly smooth – a few lumps are okay.

Mix in the crème fraîche, then season with salt and freshly ground black pepper. Transfer to a serving dish and keep warm.

Melt the butter in a small saucepan over medium heat and add the sage leaves. Continue to cook until the sage is crispy and the butter is foaming and a nut-brown colour.

Pour the mixture over the mash and serve immediately.

SERVES 4

750 g (1 lb 11 oz) cauliflower, cut into florets
375 g (13 oz) celeriac, peeled and diced
75 g (2¾ oz) crème fraîche or sour cream
75 g (2¾ oz) butter
8–10 sage leaves

NEW POTATO SALAD WITH FRESH HERBS & CRISP CAPERS

SERVES 4–6

1 kg (2 lb 3 oz) new potatoes
90 ml (3 fl oz) olive oil, plus extra for
    deep-frying
2 tablespoons red wine vinegar
2 teaspoons wholegrain mustard
2 teaspoons dijon mustard
2 tablespoons capers, drained and
    patted dry with paper towel
2 tablespoons chopped chives
2 tablespoons chopped parsley
1 tablespoon chopped basil
30 g (1 oz/1 cup, firmly packed)

Place the potatoes in a large saucepan of cold water. Bring to the boil, then reduce the heat and simmer for 15 minutes, or until cooked through. Drain and set aside.

Meanwhile, pour the 90 ml (⅓ cup) olive oil into a small bowl. Whisk in the vinegar and both the mustards, then set aside.

Heat about 1 cm (½ inch) olive oil in a small saucepan over medium–high heat, until a cube of bread turns brown in 10 seconds after being dropped in. Carefully lower the capers into the oil, standing back as they may spatter. Cook for 30 seconds, until the capers open out. Remove using a slotted spoon and drain on paper towel.

Cut the warm potatoes in half, or into slices if they are larger. Combine in a bowl with the herbs, watercress and vinegar dressing. Season to taste with salt and freshly ground black pepper, then scatter the capers over and serve.

This salad is also delicious cold, although the fried capers are best served warm.

MEDITERRANEAN TRAY BAKE

SERVES 6

10 thyme sprigs
10 rosemary sprigs, leaves picked
5 garlic cloves, peeled and smashed
250 ml (8½ fl oz/1 cup) olive oil
6–8 baby carrots
2 fennel bulbs, sliced
1 large or 2 small eggplants (aubergines),
    chopped
1 zucchini (courgette), chopped
2 red onions, each cut into 8 wedges
2 capsicums (bell peppers), cut into wedges
6 baby truss tomatoes
150 g (5½ oz) black olives
2 lemons, cut in half
100 g (3½ oz) ricotta

Combine the herbs, garlic and olive oil in a screw-top jar and shake thoroughly to combine. Set aside to infuse for 10 minutes.

Set an oven rack near the top of the oven, then preheat the oven to 215°C/420°F (fan-forced).

Arrange the carrots, fennel, eggplant, zucchini and onion in one very large roasting tin, or two smaller ones, spreading them out in a single layer, to stop them becoming soft and leaching too much liquid. Drizzle with the herbed oil mixture, then roast in the oven for 20 minutes, turning the vegetables halfway through.

Add the capsicum, tomatoes, olives and lemon halves, and gently toss to coat them in the oil. Roast for a further 20 minutes, or until the vegetables are cooked through and starting to crisp.

Transfer to a large serving platter and scatter the ricotta over.

BARBECUED CORN SALAD WITH CHIPOTLE MAYO

SERVES 4

1 tablespoon olive oil

3 corn cobs, husks and silks removed

75 g (2¾ oz/¼ cup) mayonnaise, preferably Kewpie

1¼ teaspoons chipotle sauce

3 spring onions (scallions), finely sliced

1 tablespoon chopped coriander (cilantro) leaves, plus extra sprigs to garnish

1 lime, zested, then cut into cheeks

Preheat a barbecue to medium–high heat. Brush the olive oil over the corn cobs, then place on the hot barbecue and cook for 10–15 minutes, or until the corn is cooked through, turning evenly throughout cooking so there are nice dark char marks on all sides. Remove from the barbecue and set aside until cool enough to handle.

In a small bowl, mix together the mayonnaise and chipotle sauce.

Cut the kernels from the cobs and place in a flat serving dish. Season with salt and freshly ground black pepper. Dot the chipotle mayo around the dish, then scatter the spring onions, coriander and lime zest over the top. Serve with the lime cheeks on the side.

COLCANNON

SERVES 4

1 kg (2 lb 3 oz) Dutch cream or other mashing
   potatoes, peeled
1 tablespoon olive oil
60 g (2 oz) butter
200 g (7 oz) smoked bacon, finely sliced
225 g (8 oz/3 cups) shredded white or
   savoy cabbage
3 tablespoons chopped chives

Place the potatoes in a large saucepan, cover with plenty of cold water and add a large pinch of salt. Bring to the boil, then reduce the heat and simmer for 15 minutes, or until tender.

Meanwhile, heat the olive oil and 1 tablespoon of the butter in a large frying pan over medium–high heat. Add the bacon and cook for 2–3 minutes, then add the cabbage and stir to combine. Cook for a further 5–6 minutes, or until the cabbage has wilted and the bacon is crispy.

When the potatoes are ready, drain them, then pass them through a potato ricer, back into the pan. Add the chives, remaining butter, and the sautéed cabbage and bacon mixture. Season with salt and pepper, mix well to combine, and serve immediately.

ROASTED BROCCOLI SALAD WITH PICKLED ONION

SERVES 4

500 g (1 lb 2 oz) broccoli
2 tablespoons olive oil
50 g (1¾ oz/½ cup) pecans, toasted
40 g (1½ oz/⅓ cup) dried cranberries
80 g (2¾ oz) goat's cheese, crumbled

QUICK PICKLED ONION

60 ml (2 fl oz/¼ cup) white wine vinegar
2 tablespoons sugar
1 red onion, finely sliced
125 ml (4 fl oz/½ cup) boiling water

LEMON, HERB & CAPER DRESSING

1 tablespoon chopped capers
juice of ½ lemon
2 tablespoons olive oil
½ teaspoon caster (superfine) sugar
2 tablespoons chopped mint
2 tablespoons chopped parsley

To make the quick pickled onion, place the vinegar and sugar in a heatproof bowl and stir. Add the onion, then cover with the boiling water and leave to sit for 20 minutes.

Preheat the oven to 200°C/400°F (fan-forced).

Blanch the broccoli in a saucepan of salted boiling water for 3 minutes, then refresh under cold water and drain well.

Cut the broccoli into bite-sized florets and transfer to a baking tray. Drizzle all over with the olive oil and season with salt and freshly ground black pepper.

Transfer to the oven and roast for 15–20 minutes, turning them over halfway through. Remove from the oven and keep warm.

To make the dressing, mix together the capers, lemon juice, olive oil and sugar. Add the mint and parsley, stirring to combine.

Drain the pickled onion, discarding the liquid.

Arrange the warm broccoli on a flat serving plate, then scatter over the pecans, cranberries, goat's cheese and pickled onion. Drizzle with the dressing and serve warm.

ORANGE & THYME ROASTED BABY CARROTS

SERVES 4

500 g (1 lb 2 oz) baby carrots, scrubbed
30 g (1 oz) butter
juice of ½ orange, plus the zest, cut into
    long strips using a vegetable peeler
3–4 thyme sprigs, plus extra to garnish
2 tablespoons honey
sea salt flakes, for sprinkling

Preheat the oven to 180°C/350°F (fan-forced).

Place the carrots, butter, orange juice, orange zest strips and thyme in a roasting tin large enough to fit the carrots in a single layer. Cover the roasting tin tightly with a double layer of foil.

Transfer to the oven and roast for 20 minutes.

Remove the roasting tin from the oven, and take off the foil. Drizzle the honey over the carrots.

Increase the oven temperature to 210°C/410°F (fan-forced). Roast the carrots for a further 10–15 minutes, checking once or twice, until the edges start to caramelise.

Transfer to a serving dish. Garnish with extra thyme, season with sea salt flakes and freshly ground black pepper and serve.

DESSERTS

ROASTED PEACH CAKE

✕

SERVES 8–10

6 large yellow peaches, cut into quarters
2 teaspoons melted butter
thick (double/heavy) cream or vanilla ice cream,
    to serve

CAKE

125 g (4½ oz) butter
140 g (5 oz/¾ cup, loosely packed) soft brown
    sugar, plus extra for sprinkling
55 g (2 oz/¼ cup) caster (superfine) sugar
2 large free-range eggs
finely grated zest of 1 orange
125 g (4½ oz/½ cup) plain yoghurt
2 teaspoons apple cider vinegar
150 g (5½ oz/1 cup) plain (all-purpose) flour
1 teaspoon baking powder
¼ teaspoon sea salt

Preheat the oven to 180°C/350°F (fan-forced). Line a baking tray with baking paper.

Place the peaches on the baking tray, brush lightly with the melted butter and roast in the oven for 8–10 minutes. Allow to cool.

Reduce the oven temperature to 140°C/275°F (fan-forced). Grease a 25 cm (10 inch) springform cake tin and line the base and side with baking paper.

Using a stand mixer fitted with the paddle attachment, beat the butter, brown sugar and caster sugar for 2 minutes. Scrape down the side of the bowl and continue mixing for a further 2 minutes, or until the mixture becomes lighter in colour. Add an egg and beat in well. Scrape down the side of the bowl, then add the second egg and beat for 30 seconds. Add the orange zest, yoghurt and vinegar and beat on low speed until combined.

Sift the flour, baking powder and salt together, then add to the batter in two batches, folding in with a spatula between additions.

Pour half the batter into the cake tin. Arrange half the peach pieces on top, then cover with the remaining batter. Top with the remaining peach quarters and sprinkle with an extra 1 tablespoon brown sugar. Cover the tin with baking paper and secure with ovenproof twine.

Bake for 1 hour, then carefully remove the twine and paper. Bake for a further 20 minutes, or until a skewer inserted into the middle of the cake comes out clean.

Allow to cool in the tin for 15 minutes, before removing from the tin.

Serve at room temperature, with thick cream or vanilla ice cream.

✕ This cake can be refrigerated in an airtight container, and is best enjoyed within three days.

STICKY RICE IN BANANA LEAVES WITH COCONUT JAM

MAKES ABOUT 20 PARCELS

2–3 large banana leaves, cut into 15 cm (6 inch) squares
2 ripe bananas, peeled, each cut into 10 long slices

COCONUT JAM

2 large free-range egg yolks
185 ml (6½ fl oz/¾ cup) coconut cream
75 g (2½ oz/⅓ cup) grated palm sugar (jaggery)
2 fresh pandan leaves

STICKY RICE

200 g (7 oz/1 cup) glutinous rice, rinsed and drained
250 ml (8½ fl oz/1 cup) coconut milk
pinch of sea salt flakes
50 g (1¾ oz/¼ cup) grated palm sugar (jaggery)

Start by making the coconut jam. In a bowl, whisk the egg yolks with 2 tablespoons of the coconut cream and set aside. In a saucepan, heat the palm sugar over low heat until melted. Cook, stirring occasionally, for 4 minutes, or until the sugar is a deep golden brown. Remove from the heat and cool slightly, then stir in the remaining coconut cream. Add the pandan leaves, folding them into knots to fit in the pan.

Place the pan back over low heat, stirring until smooth. Cook for 6–7 minutes, stirring, until thickened slightly. Remove the pan from the heat. Whisk the palm sugar mixture, a tablespoon at a time, into the egg yolk mixture. Pour the mixture back into the pan and cook over low heat for about 5 minutes, or until thickened. Pour through a sieve into a bowl, then cover and chill in the fridge overnight to set.

To make the sticky rice, put the rice, coconut milk, salt, palm sugar and 250 ml (8½ fl oz/1 cup) water in a saucepan, stirring well. Heat over medium heat until boiling, then reduce the heat to low and put the lid on. Simmer for 15 minutes, then remove from the heat. Rest, covered, for 30 minutes.

Soften the banana leaves over steam, or in the microwave for 30 seconds, until the leaves are soft. Place a banana leaf portion on a board, shiny side down. Spoon a tablespoon of sticky rice onto the leaf. Add a slice of banana, and a teaspoonful of coconut jam. Cover with another tablespoonful of rice, enclosing the banana and jam filling in the rice. Fold the sides of the leaves over, then roll the parcel into a cylinder. Place in a steamer basket, seam side down. Repeat with the remaining ingredients until finished, layering them in the steamer basket.

Place the steamer basket over a saucepan of boiling water. Cover and steam the parcels for 30 minutes, adding water to the steamer as necessary. Leave until cool enough to handle before removing from the steamer. Serve hot or at room temperature.

CHOCOLATE MARMALADE BREAD & BUTTER PUDDING

SERVES 4–6

9 slices pane di casa, or other similar bread,
    each about 2 cm (¾ inch) wide, cut in half
    to give 18 pieces
butter, for spreading
100 g (3½ oz/⅔ cup) chopped dark chocolate
160 g (5½ oz/½ cup) good-quality marmalade
5 large free-range eggs
170 g (6 oz/¾ cup) caster (superfine) sugar
1 teaspoon vanilla extract or vanilla bean paste
600 ml (20½ fl oz) thickened (whipping) cream
250 ml (8½ fl oz/1 cup) full-cream milk
raw sugar, for sprinkling
pouring (single/light) cream, to serve

Preheat the oven to 120°C/250°F (fan-forced). Grease a 1.75 litre (60 fl oz/7 cup) capacity shallow baking dish.

Spread one side of the bread slices with butter. Arrange in the baking dish in a couple of layers, slightly overlapping the slices, and evenly intersperse the layers with the chocolate and blobs of marmalade. Some of the marmalade can be spread on the top layer of bread.

Combine the eggs, caster sugar and vanilla in a bowl and whisk to combine. Whisk in the cream and milk until combined. Pour over the bread and leave to soak for 10 minutes, pushing the bread slices under the liquid so the crusts soften too.

Sprinkle the pudding with a little raw sugar. Place the baking dish in a large roasting tin, then pour enough very hot water into the tin to reach halfway up the side of the baking dish.

Transfer to the oven and bake for 1 hour, or until the egg mixture has just set. Carefully remove from the roasting tin and leave to cool slightly.

Serve the pudding warm, drizzled with pouring cream.

✕ The crusts on the bread give a nice texture to the pudding, but can be removed if you prefer a smoother dessert.

CRISP APPLE CRUMBLE

SERVES 4

50 g (1¾ oz) butter, plus extra for greasing
2 tablespoons caster (superfine) sugar
4 eating apples, peeled, cored and cut into
   thick wedges
1 cinnamon stick
vanilla bean ice cream, to serve

CRUMBLE TOPPING

40 g (1½ oz) soft brown sugar
75 g (2¾ oz/½ cup) plain (all-purpose) flour
25 g (1 oz/¼ cup) ground almonds
½ teaspoon ground cinnamon
25 g (1 oz) cold butter, grated

Preheat the oven to 160°C/320°F (fan-forced).

Melt the butter and sugar in a frying pan over low heat. Add the apples and cinnamon stick and cover the pan. Increase the heat to medium and cook for 4–5 minutes. Turn the apples over, then cover and continue to cook for 3 minutes, or until the apple becomes lightly caramelised.

Combine the crumble topping ingredients in a mixing bowl and mix with your fingertips until the mixture resembles crumbs.

Transfer the apples to a small buttered baking dish. Evenly sprinkle the crumble topping over the top.

Bake for 30 minutes, or until the topping is golden and the sauce underneath is bubbling.

Serve warm, with vanilla bean ice cream.

BAKED STICKY CITRUS PUDDINGS

SERVES 4

3 extra-large free-range eggs, yolks and
   whites separated
145 g (5 oz/2/3 cup) caster (superfine) sugar
finely grated zest of 1 lemon
finely grated zest of ½ orange
250 ml (8½ fl oz/1 cup) milk
75 g (2½ oz/½ cup) plain (all-purpose) flour,
   sifted
80 g (2¾ oz) butter, melted and cooled slightly
2 tablespoons lemon juice
1 tablespoon orange juice
1 tablespoon lime juice
thick (double/heavy) cream, to serve

Preheat the oven to 160°C/320°F (fan-forced). Lightly grease four 350 ml (12 fl oz) capacity mugs or baking dishes.

In a clean bowl, whisk the egg whites until soft peaks form, using an electric mixer.

In a large mixing bowl, beat the egg yolks and sugar for 10 minutes, or until pale and creamy, using an electric mixer. Add the lemon and orange zest and beat well. Gently stir in the milk, then fold in the flour.

Add the butter, all the citrus juices and the beaten egg whites, and fold in carefully to avoid beating the air out of the eggs.

Pour the mixture into the prepared dishes. Place the dishes in a baking dish half-filled with hot water.

Transfer to the oven and bake for 40–45 minutes, or until the tops have set and turned golden brown. The base will be a tangy citrus curd.

Serve the puddings hot, with thick cream.

RICOTTA & PEAR CHEESECAKE WITH A MACADAMIA CRUST

SERVES 8

3 just-ripe pears, peeled, cored and cut into quarters
600 g (1 lb 5 oz) fresh ricotta
250 g (9 oz) cream cheese, softened
125 ml (4 fl oz/½ cup) thickened (whipping) cream
1½ teaspoons vanilla bean paste or vanilla extract
2 large free-range eggs
170 g (6 oz/¾ cup) caster (superfine) sugar
sifted icing (confectioners') sugar, to serve
thick (double/heavy) cream, to serve

CRUST

250 g (9 oz) shortbread cookies
60 g (2 oz) macadamia nuts, toasted
70 g (2½ oz) unsalted butter, melted

Preheat the oven to 160°C/320°F (fan-forced). Grease a 22 cm (8¾ inch) springform cake tin and line the base with baking paper.

To make the crust, place the cookies and macadamias in a food processor and blend to coarse crumbs. Add the butter and pulse until the mixture comes together in clumps. Press into the cake tin and bake for 10 minutes.

Remove from the oven. Reduce the oven temperature to 120°C/250°F (fan-forced).

Arrange the pears, cut side down, around the crust, leaving some space in between, and finish with two pear quarters in the centre.

In a large bowl, beat the ricotta and cream cheese together until well combined. Add the cream, vanilla, eggs and sugar and beat until smooth.

Pour the mixture over the pears, smoothing to cover the fruit and give a flat surface. Bake for 55–60 minutes, or until just set.

Leave the cake in the oven with the door slightly ajar for 2 hours, or until cooled. Chill in the fridge for 3 hours, or until cold.

Dust thickly with icing sugar and serve with thick cream.

WINTER WARMING DRIED FRUIT COMPOTE

SERVES 4

90 g (3 oz) dried peach halves
90 g (3 oz) dried apricots
90 g (3 oz) dried pears
60 g (2 oz/½ cup) dried cranberries
250 ml (8½ fl oz/1 cup) verjuice (see note)
   or water
170 g (6 oz/¾ cup) caster (superfine) sugar
1 cinnamon stick
1 teaspoon vanilla bean paste
vanilla ice cream or porridge, to serve

Preheat the oven to 140°C/275°F (fan-forced).

Arrange the dried peaches, apricots, pears and cranberries in a casserole dish.

Put the remaining ingredients in a saucepan. Add 500 ml (17 fl oz/ 2 cups) cold water and stir over medium heat until the sugar has dissolved. Leave to simmer for 5 minutes.

Pour the sugar syrup over the fruit. Cover the casserole dish, transfer to the oven and bake for 1½ hours.

Serve the fruit compote with vanilla ice cream for dessert, or with porridge for breakfast. It will keep in an airtight container in the fridge for up to a week.

X Made from the juice of unripe grapes, verjuice adds a lovely dimension to this dish. If you don't have any, you could use 60 ml (2 fl oz/¼ cup) lemon juice mixed with 185 ml (6½ fl oz/ ¾ cup) water, or simply replace with water.

CHAI TEA SPICED SLOW-BAKED RICE PUDDING

SERVES 6

110 g (4 oz/½ cup) arborio rice

1 litre (34 fl oz/4 cups) full-cream milk

55 g (2 oz/¼ cup) caster (superfine) sugar

2 black tea bags (such as English breakfast)

2 cinnamon sticks

7 cardamom pods, lightly crushed

8 black peppercorns

6 whole cloves

25 g (1 oz) butter, chopped

whipped cream or thick (double/heavy) cream,
   to serve (optional)

CINNAMON SUGAR

1½ tablespoons caster (superfine) sugar

2 teaspoons ground cinnamon

Preheat the oven to 120°C/250°F (fan-forced). Grease a 1.75 litre (60 fl oz/7 cup) capacity rectangular baking dish.

Place the rice in the base of the dish. Pour the milk over and stir in the sugar. Add the tea bags, leaving the paper tags outside the dish. Add the spices and a small pinch of sea salt flakes, stirring briefly.

Cover the dish with foil and place the dish on a baking tray. Transfer to the oven and bake for 1 hour 10 minutes. Carefully remove the foil, then bake for a further 45–50 minutes. A skin may form on the top; if so, carefully remove the skin, without removing the spices.

Dot the chopped butter around the dish. Combine the cinnamon sugar ingredients and sprinkle half over the pudding. Return to the oven and bake for a further 15–20 minutes, or until slightly golden.

Gently remove any skin, as well as the tea bags and the spices. Stir and serve the creamy rice in bowls, with the remaining cinnamon sugar, and cream if desired.

✕ This pudding tastes just like chai tea. You can serve it on its own, or with poached fruit, such as pear or quince.

SLOW-BAKED SPICED QUINCES

SERVES 4–6

3 lemons

1.5 kg (3 lb 5 oz) quinces

1 orange, zest cut into wide strips

440 g (1 lb/2 cups) sugar

2 cinnamon sticks

1 vanilla bean, cut in half lengthways, seeds scraped

2 star anise

4 whole cloves

6 black peppercorns

crème fraîche or thick (double/heavy) cream, to serve

Preheat the oven to 90°C/195°F (fan-forced).

Cut the lemons in half, squeeze the juice into a large bowl of water, then add the lemon halves to the bowl.

Working with one quince at a time, peel the fruit and remove the cores, reserving the peel and cores. Cut each quince into eight wedges or pieces, immediately adding them to the bowl of lemon water so they don't brown. Wrap the reserved quince scraps in a piece of muslin (cheesecloth) and secure with kitchen string.

Pour 625 ml (21 fl oz/2½ cups) water into a heavy-based saucepan. Add the orange zest to the pan along with the juice. Add the sugar, cinnamon sticks, vanilla seeds and pod, star anise, cloves and peppercorns.

Bring to the boil, add the muslin bag and simmer for 15 minutes, or until the liquid is syrupy. Remove the muslin bag, reserving the orange rind and spices.

Drain the quince and place in a single layer in a shallow baking dish that is just large enough to hold them. Pour the syrup over, including the reserved orange rind and spices, so the syrup comes three-quarters of the way up the side of the quince. Cut a sheet of baking paper to fit over the quince pieces, to lock in the moisture as they cook.

Transfer to the oven and bake for 8 hours, or until the quince is red and tender.

Remove the baking paper and increase the oven temperature to 120°C/250°F (fan-forced). Bake for a further 20–30 minutes, or until the syrup has reduced. Remove the spices.

Serve drizzled with the syrup, with a dollop of crème fraîche. Any leftover quince will keep in an airtight container in the fridge for several days.

CINNAMON & ORANGE CRÈME CARAMELS

Preheat the oven to 120°C/250°F (fan-forced).

Combine the cream, milk, vanilla, cinnamon and orange peel strips in a saucepan. Bring just to the boil, then remove from the heat and allow to infuse for 10 minutes.

Place 230 g (8 oz/1 cup) of the sugar in a saucepan. Add 80 ml (2½ fl oz/⅓ cup) water and stir over medium heat until the sugar has dissolved. Increase the heat to high. Cook, without stirring, for 5–7 minutes, or until the caramel becomes dark golden, swirling the pan occasionally.

Working quickly, pour the caramel into six 185–250 ml (6½–8½ fl oz/¾–1 cup) ramekins or ovenproof dishes. Set aside for the caramel to set.

Place the egg yolks and eggs in a bowl and whisk in the remaining sugar. Gradually whisk in the cream mixture.

Strain the mixture into a jug, then pour the mixture into each ramekin, over the caramel. Place the ramekins in a baking dish and fill the dish with enough hot water to come halfway up the side of the ramekins.

Transfer to the oven and bake for 1 hour, or until the custards are just set. Carefully remove the ramekins from the water and allow to cool. Refrigerate for 3 hours, or until set.

To serve, run a flat-bladed knife around the inner edge of each ramekin. Place a serving plate on top of each ramekin and gently invert.

MAKES 6

375 ml (12½ fl oz/1½ cups) thickened (whipping) cream
375 ml (12½ fl oz/1½ cups) milk
1 teaspoon vanilla extract or vanilla bean paste
1 teaspoon ground cinnamon
2 orange peel strips, about 2.5 cm (1 inch) wide, pith removed
400 g (14 oz/1¾ cups) caster (superfine) sugar
7 large free-range egg yolks
2 large whole free-range eggs

ROASTED BERRIES WITH ALMOND CRUMBLE & ROSEWATER CREAM

SERVES 4

250 g (9 oz/1⅔ cups) strawberries,
    hulled and halved
150 g (5½ oz) fresh blackberries
2 tablespoons rosewater
150 ml (5½ fl oz) whipping cream
small handful mint, to garnish

ALMOND CRUMBLE

75 g (2¾ oz/½ cup) plain (all-purpose) flour
115 g (4 oz/½ cup) caster (superfine) sugar
60 g (2 oz) butter, chopped
45 g (1½ oz/½ cup) flaked almonds

Put the strawberries and blackberries in a small bowl, drizzle with 1 tablespoon of the rosewater and leave to sit for 30 minutes.

Whip the cream, mix the remaining rosewater through and set aside in the fridge until ready to serve.

Preheat the oven to 160°C/320°F (fan-forced). Line two baking trays with baking paper.

To make the crumble, combine the flour, sugar, butter and a pinch of salt in the small bowl of a food processor and pulse until the mixture resembles fine breadcrumbs. Transfer to one of the baking trays and bake for 10 minutes.

Remove the crumble mixture from the oven and add the almonds. Transfer the berry mixture to the other baking tray.

Place both trays in the oven and bake for a further 10–15 minutes, or until the crumble mixture is golden brown, and the berries are softened and lightly roasted.

If any of the crumble edges are looking a bit too brown, remove and discard them.

Divide the warm fruit and crumble among four bowls. Top each with a dollop of the rosewater cream and garnish with mint leaves.

APPLE & BLUEBERRY PIE

SERVES 8–10

40 g (1½ oz) butter, plus extra for greasing
350 g (12½ oz/2¼ cups) fresh blueberries
75 g (2¾ oz/⅓ cup) sugar, plus extra for
    sprinkling
2 tablespoons cornflour (cornstarch)
½ teaspoon ground cinnamon
3 large granny smith apples, peeled, cored
    and roughly sliced
1 free-range egg, beaten

PASTRY

460 g (1 lb) plain (all-purpose) flour
¾ teaspoon salt
315 g (11 oz) butter, cubed and chilled
30 ml (1 fl oz) iced water, approximately

Grease a 22 cm (8¾ inch) loose-based tart (flan) tin with butter.

To make the pastry, pulse the flour, salt and butter in a food processor until the mixture resembles breadcrumbs. Slowly add the water, until the mixture comes together.

Turn out onto a clean work surface and gently knead into a ball. Wrap in plastic wrap and rest the pastry in the fridge for at least 30 minutes.

Meanwhile, put the blueberries, sugar, cornflour and cinnamon in a bowl. Mix together, mashing with a fork three or four times so that a few of the blueberries break. Leave to sit on the work surface until the dough has finished resting in the fridge.

Preheat the oven to 180°C/350°F (fan-forced).

Divide the dough into two equal portions. Roll out one piece to 3 mm (⅛ inch) thick, then carefully line the tart tin, leaving any excess overlapping the sides.

Roll out the second piece of pastry to the same size, then cut it into ten strips, about 2 cm (¾ inch) wide.

Arrange the apples slices evenly over the pastry base. Evenly spoon the blueberry mixture over the apples, then dot the butter over the blueberries.

To make a lattice top for the pie, arrange five of the pastry strips evenly on top of the filling, then bend the 2nd and 4th strips up to about halfway back. Lay one strip perpendicular to the others where the bend occurs. Unfold the 2nd and 4th strips, then fold back the 1st, 3rd and 5th strips (ie, the ones you hadn't folded before). Lay another strip perpendicular at the fold, about 1–1.5 cm (½ inch) below from the last strip, then unfold the 1st, 3rd and 5th strips. Turn back the 2nd and 4th strips again, lay another strip perpendicular at the fold, about 1–1.5 cm (½ inch) below from the last strip, then unfold.

Repeat the process on the upper side of the pie, until you have a full lattice. Use a small sharp knife to trim the excess pastry from the edges. Crimp the edges together using a fork, or your thumb and forefinger.

Brush the lattice with the beaten egg, and sprinkle some extra sugar over.

Transfer to the lower rack of the oven and bake for 30–40 minutes, or until the pastry is golden brown.

Cut into slices to serve. This pie is also delicious cold.

APPLE &
BLUEBERRY
PIE
×

ROASTED WHITE CHOCOLATE DIP WITH GRISSINI

SERVES 6

200 g (7 oz) white chocolate (at least
   30% cocoa solids), broken into pieces
pinch of sea salt flakes
1 tablespoon crème fraîche, approximately

GRISSINI

150 ml (5 fl oz) lukewarm water
2 teaspoons active dried yeast
1 teaspoon sugar
300 g (10½ oz/2 cups) bread flour, plus extra
   for dusting
1 teaspoon salt
2 tablespoons olive oil, plus extra for greasing
sea salt flakes

Preheat the oven to 120°C/250°F (fan-forced). Line a baking tray with foil.

Scatter the chocolate on the baking tray and roast for 10 minutes. Remove from the oven and stir the chocolate with a spatula, mixing the browned chocolate on the bottom with the paler chocolate on top. Spread the chocolate out and pop back in the oven.

Repeat this process every 5–10 minutes, until the chocolate is a deep golden colour. Don't worry too much if your chocolate turns grainy instead of melted, as it will later be blitzed in a food processor.

Set the chocolate aside to cool completely. Turn the oven off at this point, as the grissini dough will need to prove for 2 hours.

To make the grissini, combine the water, yeast and sugar in a small jug and set aside for 10 minutes, or until bubbles appear on the surface. Place the flour and salt in a large bowl and make a well in the centre. Pour in the olive oil and yeast mixture and bring together with your hands until you have a rough dough. Knead on a lightly floured surface for 10 minutes, or until the dough is smooth and silky. Transfer to an oiled bowl, cover with a dish towel and set aside in a warm place to prove for 1 hour.

Roll the dough out into a large rectangle, about 1 cm (½ inch) thick. Cover with a dish towel and leave to prove in a warm place for a further 1 hour.

Preheat the oven to 160°C/320°F (fan-forced). Sprinkle sea salt flakes over the dough and gently run a rolling pin over top. Cut the dough into 1 cm (½ inch) thick lengths, then cut the lengths in half. Gently pull and twist each piece of dough into a stick shape. Transfer to a baking tray and bake for 20 minutes, or until light brown and crisp. Set aside to cool.

Transfer the cooled roasted white chocolate to a food processor and sprinkle with sea salt flakes. Add the crème fraîche and process until you have a smooth, thick sauce; you may need to add an extra few teaspoons of crème fraîche to get the consistency just right. Transfer to a serving bowl and serve with the grissini for dipping.

SHERRY CARAMEL FIGS WITH VANILLA MASCARPONE

SERVES 4

8 large fresh figs
100 g (3½ oz) butter
55 g (2 oz/¼ cup, firmly packed) soft brown
 sugar
2 tablespoons Pedro Ximénez, or any
 good-quality sweet sherry
250 g (9 oz) mascarpone
3 tablespoons icing (confectioners') sugar
1 vanilla bean, split lengthways and
 seeds removed
handful pistachios, roughly chopped

Preheat the oven to 200°C/400°F (fan-forced). Line a roasting tin with baking paper.

Cut the stems off the figs. Sit the figs upright in the roasting tin, then slice a deep cross in the top of each fig, nearly all the way through, but not quite – you just want the figs to open out a little to hold the sauce.

Melt the butter in a small saucepan. Remove from the heat and stir in the sugar and sherry until the sugar has dissolved. Spoon the sauce over the figs.

Transfer to the oven and roast for 10–12 minutes, or until the figs have fanned out into 'flowers' and look soft and caramelised.

Meanwhile, combine the mascarpone, icing sugar and vanilla seeds in a small bowl and whisk well until smooth and light.

Place two figs on each serving plate and drizzle with any sauce from the roasting tin. Serve with a dollop of the vanilla mascarpone, scattered with the pistachios.

CINNAMON-ROASTED PEACHES WITH FRESH RICOTTA, THYME & HONEYED HAZELNUTS

SERVES 4

70 g (2½ oz/½ cup) hazelnuts, roasted
   and peeled
2 tablespoons honey
about 3 tablespoons brown sugar
80 g (2¾ oz) butter, cut into 8 pieces
¼ teaspoon ground cinnamon
1 teaspoon thyme leaves
4 peaches, cut in half, stones removed
100 g (3½ oz) fresh ricotta

Preheat the oven to 180°C/350°F (fan-forced). Line two baking trays with baking paper.

Put the hazelnuts in a non-stick frying pan over medium heat. Add the honey and leave for 2–3 minutes, swirling occasionally so that the honey melts and covers the nuts. Transfer to one of the baking trays, separating the nuts as you go. Leave to cool, then chop roughly and set aside.

On the second baking tray, pile the sugar into eight separate little mounds, using about 1½ teaspoons of sugar for each mound, and leaving enough space in between for the peaches to sit on top.

Top each little sugar mound with a piece of butter, then sprinkle with the cinnamon. Divide half the thyme leaves among the mounds, then place half a peach, cut side down, onto each mound.

Transfer to the oven and roast for 15–20 minutes, or until the peaches are soft and the sugar has dissolved.

Divide the warm peach halves among four plates. Divide the ricotta between them, then scatter the honeyed hazelnuts and remaining thyme leaves over the top. Serve warm.

MACADAMIA DARK CHOCOLATE BROWNIES

MAKES 20

100 g (3½ oz) macadamias
175 g (6 oz) dark chocolate (50% cocoa),
    broken into pieces
125 g (4½ oz) unsalted butter
75 g (2¾ oz/½ cup) plain (all-purpose) flour
½ teaspoon salt
½ teaspoon baking powder
3 free-range eggs
125 g (4½ oz) caster (superfine) sugar
1 teaspoon natural vanilla extract

Preheat the oven to 140°C (280°F). Line a small baking tin with foil.

Spread the macadamias onto the baking tin and roast for about 15 minutes, or until golden, shaking the tin every few minutes to ensure they don't burn. Set aside to cool.

Meanwhile, bring a saucepan of water to the boil. Put the chocolate and butter in a heatproof bowl and set it over the saucepan, ensuring the bottom of the bowl isn't touching the water, and stir the mixture regularly until smooth. Remove from the heat and set aside to cool a little.

Increase the oven temperature to 160°C/320°F (fan-forced). Line a 15 cm (6 inch) square baking tin with baking paper.

Sift the flour, salt and baking powder into a small bowl.

In a large heatproof bowl, combine the eggs and sugar. Add the melted chocolate and the vanilla extract and whisk vigorously for 1 minute. Gently fold in the flour mixture, a tablespoon at a time, until thoroughly combined. Stir the toasted macadamias through.

Pour the mixture into the square baking tin and smooth the top with a palette knife. Transfer to the oven and bake for 20 minutes.

Transfer the baking tin to a wire rack and leave to cool for 10 minutes.

Remove the brownie from the tin and allow to cool completely before slicing. The brownies will keep in an airtight container for 3–4 days.

BAKED LEMON CHEESECAKE WITH RASPBERRY GLAZE

SERVES 8–10

250 g (9 oz/2 cups) fresh raspberries

BASE

180 g (6½ oz) gingernut biscuits
180 g (6½ oz) granita (digestive) biscuits
¼ teaspoon salt
150 g (5½ oz) butter, melted

FILLING

250 g (9 oz/1 cup) sour cream
550 g (1 lb 3 oz) cream cheese
115 g (4 oz/½ cup) caster (superfine) sugar
80 ml (2½ fl oz/⅓ cup) lemon juice
grated zest of 1 lemon
3 free-range eggs

RASPBERRY GLAZE

250 g (9 oz) frozen raspberries, thawed
1 tablespoon caster (superfine) sugar
1 teaspoon cornflour (cornstarch)

Preheat the oven to 140°C/275°F (fan-forced). Line the base of a 23 cm (9 inch) springform cake tin with baking paper.

To make the base, blend all the biscuits with the salt in a food processor until the mixture resembles breadcrumbs. Transfer to a bowl and mix in the melted butter. Transfer to the cake tin, pressing down so the crumbs are tightly packed over the base.

To make the filling, blend the sour cream, cream cheese, sugar, lemon juice and zest in a food processor until well combined, then add the eggs and blend again until just combined.

Pour the filling over the biscuit base. Leave the mixture to sit for 20 minutes to allow any air bubbles to rise to the surface.

Gently lift the tin and let it fall on the work surface a few times, to force out any remaining air bubbles.

Transfer to the oven and bake for 50–60 minutes, or until the filling in the middle of the cheesecake has set, but still wobbles slightly. Turn off the oven, leave the door ajar and leave to cool completely.

While the cheesecake is in the oven, make the glaze. Purée the frozen raspberries in a blender. Add the puréed raspberries to a small saucepan with the sugar and cornflour, then cook for 4–5 minutes, or until slightly thickened. Set aside to cool.

Once the cheesecake has cooled, run the edge of a knife around the outer edge of the cheesecake, just to loosen it from the the tin. Pour the raspberry glaze over the top, smoothing it out with a palette knife.

Transfer to the fridge and leave to cool for 2–3 hours, or overnight.

When ready to serve, remove from the tin and scatter the fresh raspberries over.

PEACH & BLUEBERRY COBBLER

SERVES 6

butter, for greasing
800 g (1 lb 12 oz) peaches, stones removed,
  cut into wedges (see note)
250 g (9 oz) blueberries (fresh or frozen)
80 g (2¾ oz/⅓ cup, firmly packed) soft brown
  sugar
2 tablespoons plain (all-purpose) flour
2 teaspoons vanilla bean paste
1 teaspoon ground cinnamon
½ teaspoon freshly grated nutmeg
finely grated zest and juice of 1 orange
ice cream or cream, to serve
sifted icing (confectioners') sugar, for
  dusting (optional)

TOPPING

150 g (5½ oz/1 cup) self-raising flour, sifted
40 g (1½ oz/⅓ cup) hazelnut meal
30 g (1 oz/¼ cup) rolled (porridge) oats
2 tablespoons brown sugar
100 g (3½ oz) chilled unsalted butter, grated
1 free-range egg, lightly beaten
80 ml (2½ fl oz/⅓ cup) milk

Preheat the oven to 160°C/320°F (fan-forced). Lightly butter a 1.5 litre (51 fl oz/6 cup) baking dish.

Combine the fruit, sugar, flour, vanilla, spices, orange zest and orange juice in a large bowl. Spoon into the baking dish and set aside.

To make the topping, combine the flour, hazelnut meal, oats and sugar in a large bowl. Add the butter and use your fingertips to rub the butter into the dry ingredients, until the mixture resembles coarse breadcrumbs.

In a separate bowl, whisk the egg and milk together. Add to the flour mixture and stir until the dough just comes together – do not over-mix. Spoon heaped tablespoonfuls on top of the fruit mixture, leaving small gaps between the dough.

Bake for 40–45 minutes, or until the fruit is tender and bubbling, and the topping is well browned and cooked through.

Dust with icing sugar if you like, and serve with ice cream or cream.

✗ This recipe also works beautifully with other large stone fruit – try plums or nectarines.

ROAST BANANA ICE CREAM WITH SALTED CARAMEL PECANS

MAKES ABOUT 1 LITRE (34 FL OZ)

500 ml (17 fl oz/2 cups) full-cream (whole) milk
250 ml (8½ fl oz/1 cup) whipping cream
   (35% fat)
30 ml (1 fl oz) Marsala
2 teaspoons vanilla bean paste
150 g (5½ oz/⅔ cup, firmly packed) brown sugar
5 free-range egg yolks

ROAST BANANAS

2 large ripe bananas, peeled and sliced 1 cm
   (½ inch) thick
2 tablespoons brown sugar
½ teaspoon sea salt flakes

Pour the milk, cream and Marsala into a heavy-based saucepan and add the vanilla bean paste.

Set a large bowl over an ice bath. In another bowl, whisk the sugar and egg yolks until slightly thickened.

Whisk the egg yolks into the milk mixture and place the pan over medium heat. Cook, stirring constantly, for about 5 minutes, or until the custard thickens slightly and coats the back of a spoon; it should register 85°C (185°F) on a cooking thermometer.

Strain the custard mixture into the large bowl on the ice bath, discarding any solids, and stir until cold.

Cover and refrigerate the custard until well chilled, for at least 2–3 hours, or overnight.

Preheat the oven to 180°C/350°F (fan-forced). Line a baking tray with baking paper.

To roast the bananas, spread the slices on the baking tray, in a single layer, and sprinkle with the sugar and salt flakes. Roast for about 20 minutes, until lightly caramelised and softened.

Transfer the bananas to a bowl and roughly mash with a fork. Set aside to cool, then cover and refrigerate until required.

Line another large baking tray with baking paper.

To make the salted caramel pecans, stir the sugar, butter and honey in a small heavy-based saucepan over low heat until the sugar dissolves. Increase the heat to medium and boil, without stirring, for 2–3 minutes, or until the caramel is golden brown.

Remove from the heat, add the pecans and swirl the pan to coat the pecans. Working quickly, spread the pecans over the lined baking tray and sprinkle with the salt flakes. Set aside for 30 minutes, or until cool and set, then roughly chop into pieces. (The salted caramel pecans will keep in an airtight container in the pantry for 3–4 days.)

When the custard is completely cold, churn it in an ice-cream machine according to the manufacturer's instructions.

When the ice cream begins to thicken (usually around 15 minutes), add the roasted banana and continue to churn until very thick.

Working quickly, scoop the ice cream into a chilled 1.25 litre (42 fl oz/5 cup) container, alternating with a sprinkling of the chopped caramel pecans, reserving some of the pecans to sprinkle over the top.

Return to the freezer for 2–3 hours, or until firm. Well covered or sealed, the ice cream will keep in the freezer for 3–4 days.

SALTED CARAMEL PECANS
55 g (2 oz/¼ cup) caster (superfine) sugar
40 g (1½ oz) unsalted butter, chopped
1 tablespoon honey
120 g (4½ oz) pecans
½ teaspoon sea salt flakes

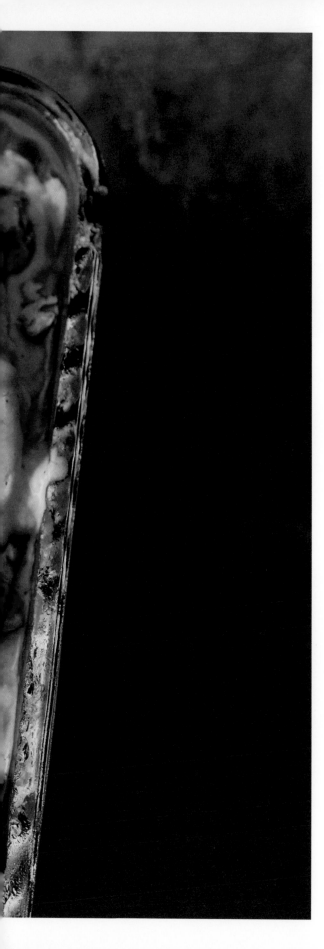

ROAST BANANA ICE CREAM WITH SALTED CARAMEL PECANS
X

DULCE DE LECHE & CHOCOLATE PEANUT BUTTER PUDDINGS

SERVES 6–8

125 g (4½ oz) butter, softened

125 g (4½ oz/⅔ cup, lightly packed) soft brown sugar

1 teaspoon vanilla extract

2 large free-range eggs

150 g (5½ oz/1 cup) self-raising flour

30 g (1 oz/¼ cup) unsweetened cocoa powder

150 g (5½ oz/1 cup) dark chocolate melts, chopped in half

125 ml (4 fl oz/½ cup) milk

180 g (6½ oz/½ cup) dulce de leche (approximately half the amount from the recipe above)

1½ tablespoons crunchy natural peanut butter (no added salt or sugar)

thick (double/heavy) cream, to serve

DULCE DE LECHE

395 g (14 oz) tin of condensed milk

Start by making the dulce de leche. Place the tin of condensed milk on its side in a large saucepan. Cover with water so it is submerged by at least 5 cm (2 inches). Bring to a simmer, then leave to simmer for 3 hours, topping up the water regularly so the tin remains completely submerged. Carefully remove the tin from the water. Allow to cool before opening. Spoon into a bowl and whisk until smooth. You'll only need about half the resulting dulce de leche for the puddings; the rest will keep in an airtight container for up to 5 days.

Grease a 1.5 litre (51 fl oz/6 cup) steamed pudding basin (mould) and line the base with baking paper. Beat the butter and sugar together in a bowl. Beat in the vanilla and eggs, one at a time, until fluffy and well combined. Sift the flour and cocoa powder together and mix in the chocolate melts. Fold into the egg mixture with the milk until combined. In a separate bowl, mix the dulce de leche and peanut butter together.

Spoon half the chocolate mixture into the pudding basin. Spoon in the dulce de leche mixture, then cover with the remaining chocolate mixture. Grease a sheet of baking paper and use it to cover the top of the pudding basin. Top with two layers of foil, then secure with string.

Fill a large saucepan one-third full of water and bring to the boil. Reduce the heat to a simmer. Place the pudding basing in the saucepan and cover with a lid. Gently simmer for 1 hour 20 minutes, or until a skewer inserted into the top of the pudding, through the foil, comes out almost clean, but a little fudgy.

Carefully remove the pudding from the water, then remove the string, foil and paper. Invert the pudding onto a plate. Slice into wedges and serve with thick cream.

ROAST CHERRY BAKEWELL TART

SERVES 10

350 g (12½ oz) pitted fresh cherries
grated zest of 1 orange
2 tablespoons soft brown sugar
120 g (4½ oz) butter
120 g (4½ oz) sugar
120 g (4½ oz/1¼ cups) almond meal
2 free-range eggs
2 tablespoons plain (all-purpose) flour
2 tablespoons flaked almonds
ice cream, to serve

PASTRY

150 g (5½ oz/1 cup) plain (all-purpose) flour
pinch of salt
60 g (2 oz) cold butter, chopped
1 free-range egg yolk
3–4 tablespoons ice-cold water

To make the pastry, combine the flour and salt in a food processor and blitz briefly. Add the butter and pulse until you have a breadcrumb consistency. Add the egg yolk and pulse a few times to combine. With the motor running, add the water, until the dough forms a ball.

Wrap in plastic wrap and set aside to rest in the fridge for 1 hour.

Roll the pastry out between two sheets of baking paper, then use it to line a 20 cm (8 inch) loose-based tart (flan) tin. Prick the base with a fork and chill for a further 30 minutes.

Meanwhile, preheat the oven to 190°C/375°F (fan-forced).

Place the cherries in a baking tin and sprinkle with the orange zest and brown sugar. Toss the mixture until well combined, then bake for about 30 minutes, or until the cherries are soft and caramelised. Set aside to cool.

Line the rested pastry shell with baking paper, then cover with baking beads, dried beans or rice. Transfer to the oven and blind bake for 10 minutes.

Remove the baking paper and beads and bake the pastry for a further 10 minutes, or until the base is light brown. Remove from the oven and set aside to cool for 10 minutes.

Reduce the oven temperature to 160°C/320°F (fan-forced).

Melt the butter in a small saucepan. Transfer to a heatproof bowl and whisk in the sugar and almond meal until well combined. Add the eggs one at a time, whisking lightly after each addition. Finally, fold in the flour.

Spoon the cherries into the tart shell. Pour the almond mixture over the top and spread evenly with a spatula. Scatter the flaked almonds over the top.

Bake for 20–25 minutes, or until the almond mixture has risen and a skewer inserted into the middle of the tart comes out clean.

Serve warm, with ice cream.

INDEX

Published in 2018 by Smith Street Books
Melbourne | Australia
smithstreetbooks.com

ISBN: 978-1-92541-886-6

CIP data is available from the National Library of Australia

Publisher: Paul McNally
Project managers: Hannah Koelmeyer & Aisling Coughlan
Editor: Katri Hilden
Recipe development: Sue Herold, Jane O'Shannessy, Caroline Griffiths,
    Aisling Coughlan & Lucy Heaver
Introduction text: Jane Price
Design concept: Daniel New
Design layout: Megan Ellis
Photographer: Chris Middleton
Art director & Stylist: Stephanie Stamatis
Food preparation: Caroline Griffiths, Sebastien Zinzan
    & Aisling Coughlan

Printed & bound in China by C&C Offset Printing Co., Ltd.

Book 59
10 9 8 7 6 5 4 3 2 1

Recipes in this book have previously appeared in *Low and Slow* and *Roast*, published by Smith Street Books in 2016 and 2017 respectively.